Backgrounds and Preparations for the Roanoke Voyages, 1584-1590

This painting by marine artist Darrell McClure shows Sir Richard Grenville's 1585 squadron as it might have appeared off Port Ferdinando or Hatorask Inlet. The *Tiger* is anchored in the center, with the *Elizabeth* coming about under full sail to the right. Shown in the background are other ships, behind which a very large storm is approaching. A small pinnace emerging from the inlet is probably attempting to get some of the crew back aboard the *Tiger* in order that it might stand out to sea during the storm. The records are full of reports of damage to ships and supplies resulting from east coast storms. Shallow waters, sandbars, and unpredictable winds have been the constant enemies of all sailors along the North Carolina coast from that day to this.

Backgrounds and Preparations for the Roanoke Voyages, 1584-1590

by

John L. Humber

Raleigh
America's Four Hundredth Anniversary Committee
North Carolina Department of Cultural Resources
1986

America's Four Hundredth Anniversary Committee

Lindsay C. Warren, Jr.
Chairman

Marc Basnight	William S. Powell	David Stick
Andy Griffith	L. Richardson Preyer	Mrs. Percy Tillett
John P. Kennedy	S. Thomas Rhodes	Charles B. Wade, Jr.
Robert V. Owens, Jr.	Harry Schiffman	Charles B. Winberry, Jr.
	Mrs. J. Emmett Winslow	

John D. Neville
Executive Director

Mrs. Marsden B. deRosset, Jr.
Assistant Director

Advisory Committee on Publications

William S. Powell
Chairman

Lindley S. Butler
Jerry C. Cashion
David Stick
Alan D. Watson

ISBN 0-86526-208-6

To My Father, Robert Lee Humber, Who Had the Vision

Contents

Maps and Illustrations

Tables

Foreword

America's Four Hundredth Anniversary Committee, formed in 1978 under the provisions of an act of the North Carolina General Assembly of 1973, was charged with recommending plans for the observance of the quadricentennial of the first English attempts to explore and settle North America. The committee has proposed to carry out a variety of programs to appeal to a broad range of people. Among these is a publications program that includes a series of booklets dealing with the history of the events and people of the 1580s.

Queen Elizabeth I of England enjoyed a reign that was for the most part peaceful. It was a period of prosperity, which saw the flourishing of a new interest in literature, religion, exploration, and business. English mariners began to venture farther from home, and in time talk began to be heard of hopes to establish naval bases and colonies in America. Men of the County of Devon in the southwest of England, seafarers for generations, played leading roles in this expansion. One of these, Walter Ralegh (as he most often wrote his name), became a favorite of the queen, and on him she bestowed a variety of honors and rewards. It was he to whom she granted a charter in 1584 authorizing the discovery and occupation of lands not already held by "any Christian Prince and . . . people." Ralegh promptly sent a reconnaissance expedition to what is now North Carolina, and this was followed in due time by a colony under the leadership of Ralph Lane. Headquarters were established on Roanoke Island. After remaining for nearly a year and exploring far afield, Lane and his men returned to England in 1586.

In the summer of 1587 Governor John White and a colony of 115 men, women, and children arrived and occupied the houses and the fort left by Lane. The brief annals of this colony are recorded in a journal kept by the governor; they tell of certain problems that arose early—but they also record the birth of the first English child in America. The journal further explains why Governor White consented to return to England for supplies. His departure was the last contact with the settlers who constituted the "Lost Colony," renowned in history, literature, and folklore.

Although a casual acquaintance with the facts of these English efforts might suggest that they were failures, such was far from the case. Ralegh's expenditures of time, effort, and resources (in which he was joined by many others, including Queen Elizabeth herself) had salutary effects for England and certainly for all of present-day America. From Ralegh's initial investment in the reconnaissance voyage, as well as from the colonies, came careful descriptions of the New World and samples of its products. The people of England, indeed of the Western world, learned about North America; because books were published based on what Ralegh's men discovered, they could soon read for themselves of the natives there and the promise of strange and wonderful new resources.

From these voyages and colonizing efforts came the conviction that an English nation could be established in America. In 1606, when another charter was about to be issued for further settlement, King James, who succeeded Queen Elizabeth at her death in 1603, called for advice from some of the men who had been associated with Ralegh. They assured the king that further efforts would surely succeed. With this the Virginia Company was chartered, and it established England's first permanent settlement in America at Jamestown.

Because of Sir Walter Ralegh's vision, England persisted. Because of England's persistence and its refusal to yield to Spain's claims to the region, the United States today enjoys an English heritage. The English common law is the basis of American law; American legislative bodies are modeled on the House of Commons with the rights and freedoms that it developed over a long period of time; America's mother tongue is English, and it is the most commonly spoken language in the world—pilots and navigators on international airlines and the controllers who direct them at airports all over the world use English. Americans also share England's literary tradition: Chaucer, Beowulf, King Arthur, and Shakespeare are America's too, and Americans can enjoy Dickens and Tennyson, as well as Agatha Christie and Dorothy Sayers. America's religious freedom is also in the English tradition, and several of this nation's Protestant denominations trace their earliest history to origins in England: the Episcopal church, certainly, but the Quakers, Baptists, Congregationalists, and Universalists as well.

America's Four Hundredth Anniversary Committee has planned many programs to direct national and even international attention to the significance of events that occurred from bases established by English men, women, and children, but notably Sir Walter Ralegh, in what is now North Carolina during the period 1584-1590. While some of the programs may be regarded as fleeting and soon forgotten, the publications are intended to serve as lasting reminders of America's indebtedness to England. Books, pamphlets, and folders covering a broad range of topics have been prepared by authors on both sides of the Atlantic. These, it is anticipated, will introduce a vast new audience to the facts of America's origins.

Lindsay C. Warren, Jr., *Chairman*
America's Four Hundredth Anniversary Committee

Acknowledgments

I want to express a debt of gratitude to my father, Robert Lee Humber, who first stirred my interest in one of the episodes wherein North Carolina stood for a brief yet significant moment on center stage in the history of Western culture. Secondly, I wish to express my sincere appreciation to William S. Powell of the University of North Carolina at Chapel Hill, who, many years ago, unselfishly shared with me the unpublished results of his research in England on the personnel involved in the Roanoke voyages and who more recently has given a great deal of time and thought to proofreading this manuscript.

I am also most grateful to Darrell McClure, the marine artist of Ukiah, California, who, while traveling through North Carolina, became so captivated with the story of the Elizabethans coming to Roanoke Island to begin a new nation that he provided several paintings to help convey a sense of what they experienced at sea in order to arrive there. Additionally, I am extremely grateful to David Beers Quinn for taking a special interest in reading this material and making numerous suggestions from the depth of his own extraordinary knowledge of the subject. I wish to thank Robert M. Topkins of the Historical Publications Section of the Division of Archives and History, who has been one of the most cooperative individuals with whom I have had the pleasure of working, for his receptiveness to numerous ideas and suggestions on my part. Lastly and most importantly, I wish to express my deepest gratitude to my wife, Jean Luffman Humber, for her ever-present support and encouragement.

Introduction

Mankind's insatiable curiosity about the unknown is reflected throughout history in repeated efforts to explore new frontiers and penetrate new fields of knowledge in spite of dangers encountered or the often severe penalties imposed by failure. The measure of success, however, is not always determined by the degree to which immediate objectives are achieved. Ideas deferred in their realization sometimes yield a far richer harvest to future generations than would result from their prompt fulfillment by allowing accumulated experiences to be critically appraised and the resulting knowledge utilized to its maximum advantage.

The sixteenth century witnessed the dawn of modern science and its revolutionary concepts in astronomy, geography, and mathematics. With the sixteenth century came the birth of a new age of discovery, which, stimulated by religious and social upheavals, generated many new horizons, challenging man's infinite capacity for accomplishment. An important participant in this unrelenting search for new knowledge, England produced its share of men of courage, vision, and imagination.

The English idea of colonization as viewed in Sir Walter Ralegh's day stemmed from nearly a century of evolving economic motives and changing political objectives. The first specific reason advanced by the English for attempting to plant a settlement in the New World appears to have been for the establishment of a halfway station along the elusive Northwest Passage to China. English prosperity relied primarily upon the development of an export trade with the East and upon its own domestic agriculture. As volatile political developments in the Near East closed many historic trade routes, new ones were sought; and belief in the existence of a passage to China by sea, either through or around America, served as a powerful impetus for English explorers and their merchant financiers. It was but a few steps from the concept of a halfway station to that of trade with the natives; to that of establishing fishing settlements or bases from which to search for and exploit new sources of raw materials England needed to become economically self-sufficient; to that of developing these sources of raw materials into settlements that could themselves become useful markets for English goods. The growth of this economic concept of colonization spanned the sixteenth century and set the stage for the awakening of North America in the seventeenth.

The fishermen who regularly plied their trade throughout the sixteenth century had no interest in the nebulous Northwest Passage and undoubtedly

The New World, 1587. This contemporary map by Francis Gaulle graphically shows the great void of detail in the northern part of the American continent, reflecting the lack of knowledge about that area. It symbolizes the continuing hopes of finding a Northwest Passage across the continent to the Pacific Ocean. From William P. Cumming, *The Southeast in Early Maps* (Chapel Hill: University of North Carolina Press, 1958), plate 13.

established temporary settlements along the shores of the northwestern Atlantic Ocean during the time they remained in the area. They fished to feed a growing European population, part of which was obliged to avoid the consumption of a certain amount of red meat under fiat of the Roman Catholic Church, and to provide whale oil for domestic use, a growing industry. In addition, Elizabethan England observed "fish days," imposed under royal edict as a means of stimulating the fishing industry.

Christianity itself provided one of a broad spectrum of motives for colonization abroad. Christianization of the heathen, for example, presented adventurous souls with a lofty motive for exploration. In England there existed as well many social pressures that prompted people to emigrate. Many had been alienated from the mainstream of English society by the shifting fortunes of being either a Catholic under the reign of Henry VIII, a Protestant under Mary Tudor, or a Catholic under Elizabeth I. Residence elsewhere easily became attractive to people in conflict with the crown during these times of uncertainty and would become increasingly so during the next several centuries. In addition, an apparent condition of overpopulation perplexed many leaders of the day, and a solution of sending the poor, the unemployed, and even convicted criminals to establish colonies in America was proposed at various times.

All of these varied reasons and compulsions for planting a colony in America were geared primarily to the temporary use of a suitable place for a specific purpose. It was not until Walter Ralegh's day that thought was seriously given in England to making a colony durable and to the problems encountered in achieving such permanency. By the early 1580s, however, after several unsuccessful attempts at planting colonies, there began to emerge the realization that political power could be enhanced by territorial expansion overseas and that this power could vastly increase England's national wealth and international political prestige and economic influence. Sir Humphrey Gilbert realized that a colony, in order to be permanent, had to be able to feed itself. Ralegh's 1585 colony under Ralph Lane attempted to do this and failed, for it was primarily a military garrison and prospecting party. From Lane's experience came the further realization that in order to be truly permanent, a colony must not only feed itself but also consist of men, women, and children who would be willing to make that colony their permanent home. What became the "Lost Colony," therefore, was the first English settlement organized with that purpose in mind.

This survey will be principally concerned with the physical preparations and financial background involved in bringing the first English colonists to American soil. Insofar as surviving evidence will permit, it is of interest to study the nature of the money and materials invested in these attempted colonizations and the personalities of those responsible. But in order to obtain a clear picture of these events, it is also essential to understand the close personal relationships that existed between the various players in this historic Elizabethan drama. Additionally, to evaluate more accurately the respective roles of these players, a consideration of the physical preparations yields a rewarding insight into costs; balanced with these figures, however, must be the income from privateering activities. To the majority of these investors, financial and material support of the expeditions was merely a business proposition, with the Spanish bullion-carrying galleons upon the high seas serving as the principal attraction.

Sir Walter Ralegh, that versatile Renaissance courtier of the Virgin Queen, was not only the foremost architect but also the leading instigator of the efforts that resulted in the English colonization of the New World. He was able, however, to share with only a few individuals, such as Richard Hakluyt, the clergyman, his vision of a British America and the monumental benefits that could ensue to the mother country. Although Ralegh's colonists failed in their aspirations to found a permanent colony on American soil or to obtain for their subscribers a continuing income from such investments, they did launch an idea that culminated in the establishment of the greatest nation of modern times. Twelve years after his last major effort to colonize "Virginia," and only five years before the founding of Jamestown in present-day Virginia, Ralegh wrote prophetically to Sir Robert Cecil, then secretary of state: "I shall yet live to see it an Inglishe nation." And so he did.

Sir Walter Ralegh. Photograph of painting courtesy National Gallery of Ireland, Dublin.

I. Ralegh and His Associates: Preliminary Steps

Elizabeth I

The Elizabethan era was characterized by the gradual evolution of policies designed to encourage English colonization in America. From her youth, Queen Elizabeth's interests were preoccupied with awareness of the physical world about her, the world of action and material accomplishments. Historian A.L. Rowse ascribes to Elizabeth an "extrovert intelligence" that vigorously encouraged any scheme that might profit her nation as well as herself and achieve power for her throne and greatness for her people. In an atmosphere permeated by Elizabeth's influence and personality, a renewed interest in American enterprises arose, and a dormant desire to expand into the New World, bringing Spain to quiescence in that region, began to assert itself. Having been restricted in such activities under the reign of Mary Tudor, Elizabeth's predecessor on the throne, adventuresome spirits now began to seize their opportunities. As this new coterie of men grew to maturity under Elizabeth's hegemony, Sir Walter Ralegh boldly made his way to leadership and prominence.

Sir Walter Ralegh

Sir Walter Ralegh belonged to a family (see Appendix A) that had long distinguished itself in English overseas exploits. His grandmother was Katherine Carew, member of another family with an impressive roster of eminent sons, one of whom was Sir George Carew, later earl of Totnes, as associate of Sir Humphrey Gilbert, and a possible investor in Ralegh's own expeditions. Sir Walter's mother, Katherine Champernoun, had descended from a lineage notable for public accomplishments from the time of the Norman wars to the reign of Henry VIII. By her first marriage, to Otho Gilbert, Katherine Champernoun had three sons: John Gilbert, Humphrey Gilbert, and Adrian Gilbert; by her second marriage, to Walter Ralegh of Fardell and Hayes, she bore two sons: Walter Ralegh and Carew Ralegh. All five of these brothers or half brothers actively participated in English overseas expansion and colonization. Sir Humphrey Gilbert and Sir Walter Ralegh both instigated and actually attempted the establishment of colonies on American shores, but of the two, only Sir Walter, probably because of the untimely death of Sir Humphrey at sea in 1583, succeeded in founding a settlement.

Between 1579 and 1583 Ralegh emerged into the limelight of royal favor, gaining prominence as a courtier and gradually winning admission to the

Queen Elizabeth I, the Virgin Queen, for whom both sixteenth-century and present-day Virginias were named. Portrait attributed to Marcus Gheeraerts the Younger; reproduced courtesy National Portrait Gallery, London.

Sir Humphrey Gilbert, half brother of Sir Walter Ralegh and Elizabethan explorer of Norumbega in the area of Newfoundland, was lost at sea in 1583 while on board the *Squirrel,* a very small ship rated at only 10 tons. When asked by crewmen of his flagship to return to the relative safety of the larger vessel before a storm broke, he refused, answering that one was as close to heaven by sea as by land. The *Squirrel* and Gilbert disappeared during the night. Engraving from Donald Barr Chidsey, *Sir Walter Raleigh, That Damned Upstart* (New York: John Day Company, 1931), facing p. 246.

queen's small circle of intimate friends, upon whom she lavished pensions and sinecures yielding sizable incomes. In May, 1583, Ralegh received one of his first such rewards, a grant giving him a monopoly for the issuance of licenses to sell wine. From this source of revenue he at first received some £700 to £800 per year, which later increased to as much as £1,300 per year. Additional recognition came Ralegh's way, and his prestige continued to increase. In 1584 he was given licenses to export cloth without legal impediments, and during the next few years he managed the customs on this commodity for a pension of £2,000 per year. Elizabeth also conferred upon her rising favorite such titles as lord warden of the stannaries of Cornwall, lord lieutenant of Cornwall, and vice admiral of Cornwall and Devonshire, all income-producing offices. In 1587 she selected Ralegh to fill the coveted post of captain of the Queen's Guard. The highest sign of royal esteem, however, was bestowed upon Ralegh on January 6, 1585, when Elizabeth knighted him, signifying her approval of his plans for the English colonization of the New World as well as her pleasure with the report submitted by the captain of his first expedition to the American continent. In addition to these rewards, Ralegh was granted a number of estates confiscated by the crown, and in 1587 he was assigned a plantation of some 42,000 acres of arable land in Ireland.

All these positions placed sizable funds at Ralegh's command. As lord warden of the stannaries of Cornwell, for example, he assumed responsibility for the operation of the Cornish tin mines and administered judicial and legislative functions in those mining areas. Ralegh engaged in these activities at a time when fees were customarily charged for such services. As vice admiral of Cornwell and Devonshire, Sir Walter, with his half brother, Sir John Gilbert, as his deputy, controlled the shipping in those provinces and reaped shares of profit from all privateering ventures of the South West.

This very brief review of Sir Walter Ralegh's early career identifies the principal sources of his wealth, suggests the extent of the funds at his command, and indicates the scope of his growing influence.

Richard Hakluyt, Clergyman

It was while a student at Oxford University that Ralegh probably entered into the first of a series of associations that later formed the nucleus of those persons who shared with him his vision of an English overseas empire. Richard Hakluyt, the clergyman, born perhaps in the same year as Ralegh, entered Christ Church, the leading college at Oxford, in 1570, receiving his Bachelor of Arts degree in 1574 and his Master of Arts degree in 1577. Ralegh, having attended Oriel College intermittently from approximately 1572 to 1574, was quite possibly introduced to him there. Upon leaving Oxford, Hakluyt had already acquired a great ardor for the adventures and discoveries of the earlier ocean voyagers. By 1582 he had published his first account of them in his *Divers voyages,* thereby earning the patronage of Lord Howard of Effingham, who later became lord high admiral of England and a possible investor in the Roanoke expeditions. Howard's brother-in-law, Sir Edward Stafford, became the English ambassador to France in 1583, taking Hakluyt with him to France as chaplain to the embassy. This post was probably granted as a result of Hakluyt's dedication of his *Divers voyages* to his close friend and Oxford schoolmate, Sir Philip Sidney, son-in-law to Secretary of State Francis Walsingham, who had encouraged Hakluyt in his collection of materials. It is also interesting to note that Walsingham had been previously associated with the Gilbert voyages.

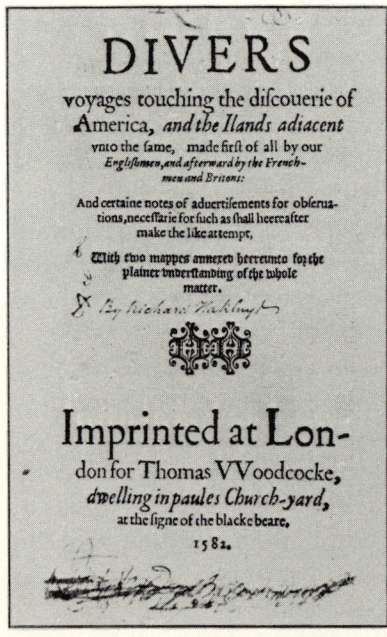

Title page from Richard Hakluyt's *Divers voyages,* his first collection of mariners' reports from overseas voyages. Title page of Chalmers copy reproduced courtesy trustees of the British Museum, London.

4

Hakluyt's duties in Paris undoubtedly included the gathering of documentation of attempts by various nations to engage in western colonization. These pursuits coincided with Ralegh's interest in western colonies, and Hakluyt became what Henry Stevens characterized as the "mouthpiece of a snug family party all playing into the hands of Raleigh." Perhaps Hakluyt's most significant contribution to this end was his successful solicitation of various authors, such as Martin Basanier, Theodor de Bry, and John Hooker, to dedicate to Ralegh their works on western colonization; in so doing, Hakluyt became the guiding spirit of the publicity campaign for the Virginia voyages. In writing to Sir Walter from Paris in 1586, Hakluyt implied the deliberate use of these inscriptions primarily as propaganda. With regard to the dedication to Ralegh of his Latin edition of Peter Martyr's *De orbe novo . . . decades octo* (1587), Hakluyt invited additional comment, declaring: "if there be any thinge else that yow would have mentioned in the epistle dedicatorie, yow shal doe wel to let mee understand of yt betymes."

Thomas Harriot

A second contact established by Ralegh was with a man some eight years his junior who remained a confidential assistant and a devoted friend until Ralegh's death in 1618. Thomas Harriot took his Bachelor of Arts degree from St. Mary's Hall, Oxford, in 1580 and immediately exhibited a marked talent for mathematics and science. He may have been introduced to Ralegh by Richard Picot, who is believed to have been Ralegh's tutor after Ralegh left Oxford. Harriot entered Ralegh's service, becoming a member of his household soon after terminating his studies at Oxford, certainly by 1583. His duties were to instruct Ralegh and Ralegh's sea captains in the sciences of astronomy and navigation. As plans for the Virginia settlement began to

Thomas Harriot, the author of *A brief and true report of the new found land of Virginia*, was a noted English mathematician who gave algebra its modern method of notation. Engraving of Harriot by Francis Delaram, 1620; reproduced courtesy trustees of the British Museum.

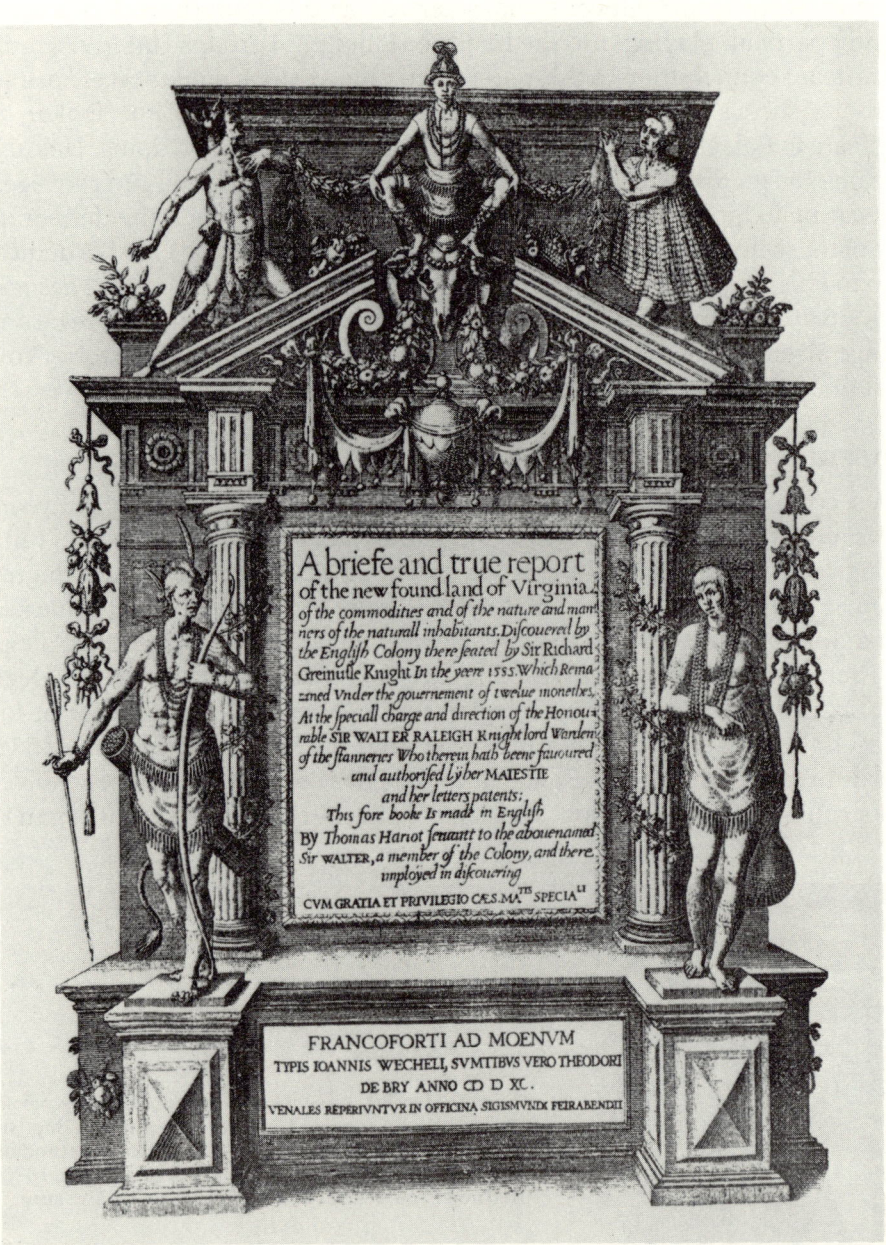

The title page of Thomas Harriot's *A briefe and true report,* the first book written about the area that is now North Carolina, described the Indians of the eastern coastal area, their life-style, and their natural environment. Photograph reproduced courtesy British Library Board, London.

take shape, Harriot prepared the instructions for the 1584 voyage of Philip Amadas and Arthur Barlowe. Subsequently, he learned the Algonquian language from the two Indians brought back to England by that first reconnaissance expedition. He probably taught the Indians some English, but he also learned a great deal about their way of life before participating in the second expedition in 1585.

Harriot's principal assignments during this voyage were to direct the colony's Indian affairs, make astronomical observations, act as navigational consultant, supervise the mapping of the discovered areas, and report on the physical and economic assets of the new land. After returning to England, but probably prior to the departure of the 1587 colony, he wrote his famous *briefe and true report of the new found land of Virginia* (1588), which includes a survey of the economic and natural resources of the Roanoke Island area and an account of the manners and customs of the Indians who lived there. In this book he demonstrated a sincere effort on his part to minister the gospel to these primitive people and described their favorable reception of the Christian doctrine.

Apart from his association with the Virginia enterprises, Harriot made his mark on the intellectual and scientific world of his day. He developed methods of geometrical computation; he virtually gave to algebra its modern form as a mathematical language; he applied optics to the exploration of the heavens in the form of a telescope, simultaneously with Galileo; and he is believed to have been the intellectual leader of the Sir Walter Ralegh-Christopher Marlowe literary circle. The importance and value of his contributions to the eventual success of a permanent English colony on American soil are immense.

John White

Another member of this intimate group surrounding Sir Walter Ralegh was John White, remembered as an eminent artist and governor of the 1587 colony. Apart from his associations with the Virginia enterprises, very little is known concerning White's life. Some questions have been raised as to whether the artist and the governor were actually the same person; however, these suspicions have been dispelled beyond any reasonable doubt. For instance, in 1593 White noted that the 1590 voyage was his fifth and last journey to Roanoke Island. This statement indicates that he must have been with Amadas and Barlowe as well as a member of Ralph Lane's colony in 1585. He was, of course, governor of the 1587 colony, and his two attempts in 1588 and 1590 to find and rejoin the 1587 settlers would account for his fourth and fifth voyages. White's name, however, does not appear in the official list of 1585 colonists, although there is a passing reference to "John White" in the *Tiger*'s journal entry of July 11, 1585, as being present in one of the boats that accompanied Sir Richard Grenville in his explorations across Pamlico Sound.

Additionally, Theodor de Bry, in his 1590 edition of *America,* Part I, stated that Ralegh had sent John White to the New World in 1585 and 1588 (probably meaning 1587) for the purpose of making the drawings that de Bry had subsequently engraved, thereby indicating no doubt in his mind that the artist and the governor were the same man. In the manuscript of Thomas Moffett's great work on insects, *Insectorum . . . theatrum,* there appears, over a drawing of a swallowtail butterfly identical to one known to have been drawn by John White, the following inscription in Latin: "White the painter brought this to me from American Virginia in 1587." And finally, in his narrative of the 1590 voyage, White speaks of his return to Roanoke Island, where he found "the frames of some of my pictures and Mappes rotten and spoyled with rayne." Thus, the identity of the artist and the governor appears to have been one.

Through his watercolor drawings, White left the earliest visual record of the Indians, flora, and fauna of the North Carolina coast, providing at the same time priceless documentation illustrating Harriot's written report on the social life of the natives and the natural resources in the region. In 1585 White's main function was to draw what he saw and map the areas discovered. His style is revealed through his map of the fort in Puerto Rico, which offers a three-dimensional aspect of the people and activities there, much as an artist might be led to show, as well as a flat plan outlining the fort, such as a surveyor might be expected to prepare. Certainly, his map of North Carolina, which he and Harriot surveyed, reflects a high degree of cartographic skill. Although most authorities view White's training as mainly that of an artist, illustrator, or illuminator of manuscripts rather than as a surveyor or cartographer, recently discovered facts about his life in Ireland after 1590 suggest the contrary. In any case, he is better remembered for his artistic contributions than for any technical competence in mathematics or draftsmanship.

As an artist, historian David Beers Quinn observes, White lends a "remarkable quality of fidelity to almost all his human figures, and a combination of grace and accuracy to the majority of his other drawings. This delicate naturalism sets White apart from all other English draughtsmen of his time, and places him as a significant artist." Upon examination of White's map of the North Carolina coast, anyone familiar with the geography of the area can easily observe, along with Quinn, that "quality of fidelity" and "accuracy" in White's cartographic work.

John White belongs historically to that small group of eminent sixteenth-century Englishmen that includes Richard Hakluyt and Thomas Harriot—not only because of his prominent role in the Virginia episode but also because of the status he acquired in his own right as a leading contributor to English cultural history. The last known correspondence from John White was during his residency in Ireland, where he was possibly managing one of Ralegh's estates. From there he wrote Hakluyt in 1593, sending him the narrative of his 1590 voyage.

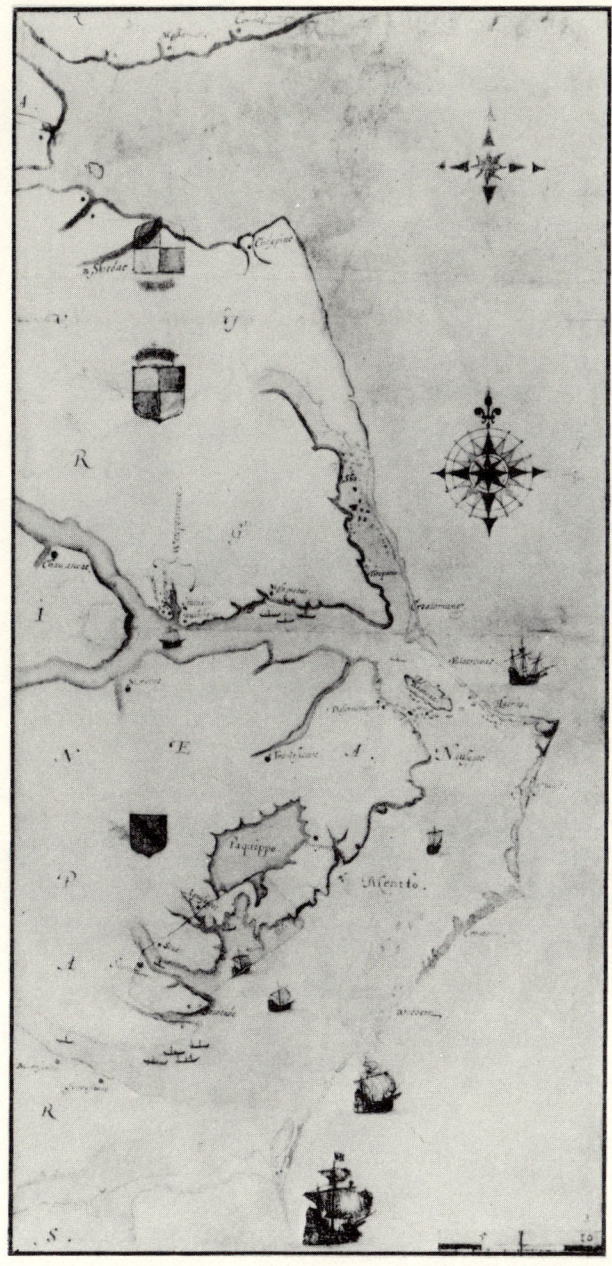

John White's map of the North Carolina coast around Roanoke Island reflects the fidelity of his observations when compared to a present-day map of the area. The large cape shown just slightly south of Roanoke Island was known as Cape Kenrick (thought to be a derivative of an Indian word meaning "sinking-down sand"), which has long since disappeared but is still present to some extent as Wimble Shoals off the present coastline. Map reproduced courtesy trustees of the British Museum.

This watercolor by John White depicts various methods of fishing employed by the Indians of Elizabethan Virginia. Reproduced courtesy trustees of the British Museum.

Richard Hakluyt, Lawyer

There remain two other notable personalities associated with Sir Walter Ralegh in his Virginia expeditions: Richard Hakluyt of the Middle Temple, lawyer and elder first cousin to Richard Hakluyt, the clergyman; and Jacques le Moyne de Morgues, artist. Richard Hakluyt of the Middle Temple is connected with the Virginia story primarily through a pamphlet, possibly written at Ralegh's request, entitled "Inducements to the liking of the voyage intended towards Virginia." This tract, in the form of a prospectus and not printed until 1602, was written in 1585, the year following the appearance of a longer pamphlet on the same subject by Hakluyt's cousin. The elder Hakluyt had previously acted as a colonial adviser to Sir Humphrey Gilbert in 1578 and to some of the English merchant companies trading with the Far East and the Levant.

Jacques le Moyne de Morgues

Jacques le Moyne was one of the survivors of the René de Laudonnière colony, which was established in Spanish Florida by the French and destroyed by the Spanish in September, 1565. An artist himself, he left numerous paintings relating to the Laudonnière colony (his widow sold the paintings to de Bry in 1588). Le Moyne had escaped the 1565 massacre in Florida and somehow made his way to France, going as a Huguenot refugee to England and Wales in 1572 and entering Ralegh's service, possibly as early as 1582 or 1583. He was lodged at Blackfriars in London under the name of James Morgan and soon gained a reputation as a bookseller and teacher as well as an artist. There is some evidence that le Moyne and John White collaborated on American subjects. Two of White's drawings of Florida Indians are copied from le Moyne, and White probably also made use of le Moyne's map of Florida in preparing his own map of eastern North America. Richard Hakluyt, in the dedication to Ralegh of his translation of Laudonnière's *L'histoire notable de la Floride* (1587), stated that Ralegh caused the Florida drawings to be done at his "no small charges by the skillful painter James Morgues, yet living in the Blackfryers in London." Le Moyne, although not important to the Virginia voyages, was a part of Sir Walter's inner circle and quite possibly had some influence on Ralegh's shifting the site of his plantation southward from Gilbert's Norumbega, in the vicinity of Newfoundland, nearer to the Florida latitudes.

These four men—Richard Hakluyt the clergyman, Thomas Harriot, John White, and Jacques le Moyne—formed an inner circle about Ralegh, actively supporting his interests and projects in whatever manner they manifested themselves. In his biography of Thomas Harriot, Henry Stevens wrote: "When Wingandacoa (Virginia) makes up her jewels she will not forget these four, whom it is just to call Raleigh's Magi."

Sir Ralph Lane

Sir Ralph Lane, governor of the first colony in 1585, did not belong to Ralegh's intimate social group of lifelong friends, nor was he one of Sir Walter's business associates. He was primarily a soldier and, as will be discussed hereafter, was part of the queen's own contribution to the 1585 expedition. Lane lived the life of a soldier, having served the crown on the high seas and in Ireland for twenty years prior to 1585. His admission into the queen's service may have had something to do with the fact that his mother, Maud Parr, was a first cousin to Catherine Parr, last queen of Henry VIII. It is also known that Lane served in Parliament in 1558 and 1563. In 1585 he was not only governor of the first colony left on Roanoke Island but was also lieutenant of the entire expedition under Sir Richard Grenville, sailing with him aboard the admiral, a name customarily applied to the flagship of a fleet in the sixteenth century. Lane's friendship of long standing with Sir Philip Sidney and his family, as well as his military ability and experience, may well have prompted his appointment. That he was a recognized authority on the art of fortification and defense is illustrated by his assignment while serving as a member of the Council of War in 1587 to survey and outline the measures necessary for the defense of the English coast against the Spanish Armada. He served with Ralegh and Grenville on this council and was the only member who had not yet been knighted. After the Armada had been repulsed, he was appointed muster master under Sir Francis Drake in 1589 and under Sir John Hawkins in 1590, and muster master general of Ireland in 1591, acting in that capacity during the Irish rebellion of 1593-1594. On October 15, 1593, after having been seriously wounded in this campaign, he was knighted by Sir William Fitzwilliam, lord deputy of Ireland. The brief interlude represented by his governorship of Virginia constituted merely another assignment in a very full military career.

William Sanderson

Sir Walter Ralegh's business associates in the Virginia expeditions varied during the seven years, 1584-1590, when he was primarily occupied with those voyages. One thing seems clear, however: in that age of kinship consciousness, Ralegh moved whenever and wherever possible within the bounds of family ties. William Sanderson, a London merchant, became a general finance manager for Ralegh and acted as a direct link with the merchant adventurers of London. Sanderson came to know Ralegh and to become closely associated with him in 1584 or 1585 through his marriage to Margaret Snedall, the daughter of Ralegh's half sister, Mary, and Hugh Snedall, a commander in the queen's Royal Navy. Whether the union was instigated by Ralegh or Sanderson, negotiated for reasons of political or commercial expediency, or simply a fortunate result of mutual affection is not known. It is certain, however, that the marriage was highly beneficial to both men: for Ralegh as a valuable tie with the mercantile element of London society, and for Sanderson as a means of indirect access to the queen's ear at court.

This relationship led to the formation of a partnership between Ralegh and Sanderson, the latter being responsible for soliciting sizable investments in Ralegh's projects.

Sanderson's cooperation with Ralegh did not end with dealings of a financial nature. Not being endowed with scholarly gifts, as were Ralegh, Hakluyt, and Harriot, Sanderson patronized those who were. Some of the men Sanderson supported were introduced to him through Hakluyt and Harriot. Robert Hues, an eminent English geographer and mathematician, for example, was an intimate friend and associate of Harriot and is known to have received financial aid from Sanderson. Sanderson likewise helped finance the Wright Molyneux globes, the first geographical globes made in England employing all the knowledge available from the voyages of John Davis in search of the Northwest Passage in the mid 1580s; the Virginia expeditions; and other ventures. Thomas Hood, a contemporary English mathematician, astronomer, and geographer, was another beneficiary of Sanderson's philanthropy. Sanderson and Ralegh ultimately quarreled over the finances involved in the latter's Guiana expeditions in the 1590s, however, and their association terminated during a heated argument.

The Royal Patents

Following the death of Sir Humphrey Gilbert in 1583, the leading contenders in attempting to secure from the crown his patents, or franchises, for colonization in the New World were Sir Walter Ralegh, Sir George Peckham, Christopher Carleill, and Sir Philip Sidney. Ralegh, through his influence at court and his relationship to Gilbert, was able to obtain, on March 25, 1584, patents virtually identical to those Queen Elizabeth had previously granted to Gilbert, including the exclusive rights to plant on "such remote heathen and barbarous Landes Contries and territories not actually possessed by any Christian Prynce and inhabited by Christian people. . . ." He was

Christopher Carleill, a contender for Sir Humphrey Gilbert's patents. Engraving from Charles W. Porter III, *Fort Raleigh National Historical Site, North Carolina* (Washington, D.C.: National Park Service, 1952), p. 16.

granted all royalties, franchises, commodities, and jurisdictions over such places he colonized, the queen reserving her own customary share of any income derived as well as her ultimate sovereign authority.

In a maneuver designed to strengthen further his monopoly on colonizing ventures as well as to eliminate the opposition, Ralegh arranged for the marriage of his first cousin, Barbara Gamage, heiress to certain large estates, to Robert Sidney, the younger brother of Sir Philip Sidney. Sir Philip was the nephew of the earl of Leicester, a powerful figure at court, and son-in-law of Sir Francis Walsingham, the secretary of state. Christopher Carleill, one of the contenders for Gilbert's patents, was a second son-in-law to Walsingham. This artful strategem, executed with a certain diplomatic cunning,

Sir Philip Sidney (left) was another contender for Sir Humphrey Gilbert's patents. Portrait, painted about 1577, reproduced courtesy National Portrait Gallery, London. Sir Francis Walsingham, secretary of state and probable investor in the Virginia ventures, is shown at right. Portrait reproduced courtesy National Portrait Gallery, London.

gathered within the Ralegh family circle Elizabethan England's most powerful exponents of American colonization and concentrated their efforts and influence in one direction under the strong leadership of Sir Walter Ralegh. Sir George Peckham, the only remaining serious contender for royal sanction, who also happened to be a Catholic, found this formidable alliance impenetrable and simply faded from the scene.

The Parliamentary Bill

Having either aligned or eliminated his opposition, Sir Walter Ralegh next sought a means by which he could draw the maximum attention to his project—not only from the wealthy government leaders, from whom he hoped to obtain at least official cooperation if not financial participation, but also from the general public, from whose ranks the colonists would be

14

chosen. He decided upon having introduced into Parliament a bill that, if passed, would give further official approbation to the patents he had already been granted by the royal prerogative. This additional confirmation does not appear to have been necessary, however, since Ralegh proceeded with his project in spite of the failure of the House of Lords to concur with the House of Commons in the passage of his bill. But it did afford a splendid means of advertisement. Whatever Ralegh's expectations of acquiring new associates might have been, they must have been richly gratified. The bill was referred for consideration to a House of Commons committee, the membership of which appears to have been packed with sympathetic minds and with a number of future supporters of the venture. The fact that Ralegh was himself a member of Parliament from Devonshire may have had some bearing upon the favorable manner with which the bill was received in Commons.

The chairman of the committee was Sir Christopher Hatton, who also was vice-chamberlain to the crown and an investor in a number of overseas voyages. Other members included Sir Francis Walsingham, a subscriber to the first colony; Sir Philip Sidney, a possible investor; Sir Francis Drake, then preparing an expedition against the Spanish West Indies; Sir Richard Grenville, a kinsman of Ralegh and later the general in the 1585 expedition; Sir William Courtenay, with Ralegh a member of Parliament from Devonshire; and William Mohun, with Grenville a member of Parliament from Cornwall.

Other members of Parliament who were brought into contact with Ralegh's project at this time were: Sir George Carey, possibly associated with the 1585 colony, who was governor of the Isle of Wight and vice admiral of Hampshire, and who married the cousin of Edmund Spencer, one of Ralegh's warmest friends; Thomas Digges, a member of Parliament from Southampton; Fulke Greville, Sir Philip Sidney's associate, representing the borough of Hedon; James Erisey, Grenville's cousin; Edward and Henry Unton, early acquaintances of Ralegh while he was at Oxford; Humphrey Prideaux, who had a kinsman who accompanied Lane in 1585; and George Carew, first cousin to Ralegh's mother, previously mentioned. Also serving in Parliament at this time were Carew Ralegh, Sir Walter's brother, and Robert Sidney, the younger brother of Sir Philip, who had married Ralegh's cousin. Only two members of Parliament actually served as members of the Grenville expedition, however: Anthony Rowse and the adventurous Thomas Cavendish, with only the former remaining as a colonist with Lane.

Sir Richard Grenville

The most important of all these associations for the Virginia voyages was the acquisition of Grenville's services. Sir Richard Grenville was Sir Walter Ralegh's distant cousin. Both men had been reared in the same seafaring tradition, and each had practically paralleled the other's military career without ever actually crossing paths. It is not known when or how Grenville was first approached to lead the 1585 expedition, or if, indeed, he

Sir Richard Grenville, kinsman of Sir Walter Ralegh, served as both admiral and general of the 1585 expedition. Portrait, 1571, reproduced courtesy National Portrait Gallery, London.

volunteered, although there is some evidence that he was a second choice, Sir Philip Sidney having already rejected the offer. After the satisfactory action on Ralegh's bill in the House of Commons, there is no evidence of Grenville's participation in any further deliberations, presumably because of his departure for the West Country in order to raise shipping and personnel, which included John Arundell, his half brother, and John Stukeley, his brother-in-law.

These foregoing relationships reveal Sir Walter Ralegh as something of a forceful and skilled diplomat, meticulously planning each move before its execution. Beginning at Oxford, he mustered about him over a period of fourteen years a group of men with brilliant minds who collaborated with him in his studies and projects and upon whom he could rely as close friends. When the opportunity to launch his plan for the colonization of the New World presented itself, he maneuvered his opponents into becoming allies, subtly securing their ardent support. It is on the basis of these associations that the Roanoke voyages were planned, prepared, and financed.

II. Personnel of the Expeditions

The 1585 Colony and Related Expeditions

The seven expeditions to Roanoke Island fall into two distinct and separate efforts at colonization: those concerned with the 1585 colony and those related to the "Lost Colony" of 1587. Associated with the first settlement are the Amadas and Barlowe exploratory venture of 1584; the actual colonizing expedition of 1585 under Sir Richard Grenville and Ralph Lane; the abortive 1585 voyage of the supply squadron under Bernard Drake of Ashe, a cousin of Sir Francis Drake, which was diverted by the queen to the Newfoundland fishing banks; and the 1586 voyages, including Sir Walter Ralegh's supply ship and Grenville's reinforcement fleet, which deposited a party of fifteen men at Roanoke Island upon finding the 1585 colony gone.

Little is known about the personnel comprising the 1584 expedition, the only source of contemporary information being Arthur Barlowe's own narrative of the voyage, which reveals little concerning personnel. Apart from Amadas and Barlowe, commanders of the expedition, there were listed eight members of the two ships' companies and two Indians—Manteo and Wanchese—who were taken to England on the return voyage. John White is also believed to have been a member of this expedition, primarily because of his statement in 1593 that he had made five voyages to Virginia. John and Benjamin Wood were listed by Arthur Barlowe as members of the company; both later achieved distinction, the former as a jurist, being knighted in 1603, and the latter as a sea captain. Henry Greene, another member of the expedition, was apparently a graduate of Corpus Christi College, Cambridge, and may possibly figure in the ancestry of General Nathanael Greene, American Revolutionary War hero. Barlowe asserted in his report that he was well provided with men, but later expressed the hope that Ralegh would be satisfied with the results of their voyage in view of the "small meanes, and number of men we had." It can only be assumed that, apart from the presence of White and possibly Greene, no other members of the 1584 venture possessed any particular talents or experience valuable for such an undertaking.

Substantial planning, however, appears to have taken place respecting the qualifications of the colonists to be sent to the New World in 1585. In his *Discourse of Western Planting,* written in 1584-1585, Richard Hakluyt, the preacher, proposed that such an overseas settlement would offer a means of unburdening England's bulging jails of indolent and mutinous subjects, for whom no occupation had existed: "Whereas yf this voyage were put in execution, these pety theves might be condempned for certen yeres in the westerne partes. . . ." But such a proposal seems to have been advanced primarily to solicit the queen's support, for in his last chapter, which lists "some things to be prepared for the voyage," Hakluyt fully describes the artisans and tradesmen that would be needed. He divided personnel requirements into six separate categories: men charged with the production of victuals; men "tending to force," that is, to defense and its related functions; personnel "incident to the first traffique and trade of merchandize"; artisans used in building; "artisans, serving our firste planters, and in parte for traffique"; and others not included in the above classifications.

This enumeration of craftsmen indicates a rather comprehensive anticipation of activities normally pursued in a community located in an area requiring defense from a neighboring foe. Of those workmen designated for the purpose of trade, the most prominent—such as pitch and tar makers, carpenters, "millwrites," and "grubbers and rooters up" of trees—reflect a primary concern with the lumber and naval stores industries, while the inclusion of other occupations—such as burners of ashes for soap, coopers for barrels, tallow makers, and dyers to seek the valuable cochineal—suggests a desire to develop primary industries in the colonies. As an overall consideration in the choice of personnel, Hakluyt cautioned that "this general rule were goodd to be observed, that no man be chosen that is knowen to be a Papiste, for the speciall inclynation they have of favour to the Kinge of Spaine."

In an unpublished memorandum entitled "Inducements to the liking of the voyage intended towards Virginia," Richard Hakluyt, lawyer and elder cousin of the clergyman, also proposed that the types of tradesmen described above be taken; however, he set forth a more detailed explanation than his clergyman cousin concerning how such tradesmen were to be employed. One such proposal is especially noteworthy: "A skillful painter is also to be caried with you, which the Spaniards use in all their discoveries to bring the description of all beasts, birds, fishes, trees, townes & c."

Also extant is a set of "Anonymous Notes For The Guidance of Raleigh and Cavendish" (the Cavendish notes), which were probably written before early January, 1585, inasmuch as they make no mention of the knighting of Ralegh, which occurred at that time. These notes, written by a military authority, possibly Sir John Smythe, Sir Roger Williams, or Thomas Digges, present a complete analysis of the organization required for a military garrison to be stationed in the wilderness. The author of these notes, endorsing them as having been "giuen to Master Candishe," recommended that the expedition be directed by a general supported by an admiral and two justices. The other officers were to be a colonel, a sergeant major, a marshal, and seven captains, the usual ranks in a military force of that epoch. The total number of men suggested was 800, to be allocated as follows: 400 harquebusiers; 100 swordsmen with light shields; 150 longbowmen; 100 men equipped with light Milan corselets and pikes; and 50 men armed with light corselets and other weapons such as halberds, bills, or battle-axes (see Appendix C). Among the tradesmen suggested as desirable to accompany the 1585 expedition, the author of these anonymous notes listed a geographer, painter, physician, surgeon, apothecary, alchemist, and lapidary in addition to those occupations previously mentioned. According to one of his biographers, Ralegh formulated a set of rules for the political organization of the colony; however, it is no longer extant.

The eventual choice of this type of colony for the 1585 venture suggests that Ralegh had either already determined that a military expedition was the most desirable means of establishing a permanent colony or that he had been so persuaded. Whether or not this decision was made as a result of the Cavendish notes, it seems fairly certain that this plan must have been adopted by February 8, 1585, when Elizabeth wrote to the lord deputy of Ireland, Sir John Perrot, asking him to release Ralph Lane, a professional soldier (who also happened to be her kinsman) for other duty she had in mind for him. Lane, of course, became governor of the 1585 colony. There is, among the contemporary documents, only one reference implying that the colony was specifically designed as a military garrison, perhaps established to operate as a privateering base.

When the expedition was actually organized, there was a marked adherence to the recommendations made in the Cavendish notes. Sir Richard Grenville served as both general and admiral of the force. Thomas Cavendish, while serving as captain of the *Elizabeth,* supported Grenville as high marshal; and Philip Amadas, formerly captain of the 1584 venture, was appointed vice admiral, remaining in the colony as admiral of Virginia. Under Cavendish, Ralph Lane and Francis Brooke served as lieutenant and treasurer respectively, while the naturalized Portuguese Simon Fernandes assisted Amadas as chief pilot. To this group was added the captains of the remaining ships[1] and five others to form a council. Prior to Grenville's departure for England, he promoted Lane to general in command of those Englishmen left by Grenville to defend Roanoke Island. Brooke, who returned home with Grenville, apparently appointed a vice-treasurer, although no record of this officer's name has survived.

In his narrative of the colony, written during the following year, Lane spoke of his "Colonel of the Chesepians," in which role Amadas, or perhaps even Harriot, possibly doubled. Lane referred to his sergeant major, whose duty it was to assemble the soldiers in battle order—but again no name was given. At various points in this narrative he mentioned his vice-treasurer, appointed by Brooke; his "master of the victuals"; and the "keeper of the store," who probably was Thomas Harvey. As a military leader, Lane emphasized strict discipline as a means of avoiding sickness and annihilation and described

---

[1]The captains of the ships were: John Clark aboard the *Roebuck,* George Raymond aboard the *Lion,* perhaps Arthur Barlowe aboard the *Dorothy,* and Cavendish aboard the *Elizabeth.* Grenville, Amadas, and Lane were aboard the *Tiger.*

Sir Thomas Cavendish, high marshal of the 1585 expedition, captain of the *Elizabeth*, and probable investor in the venture. Engraving from Henry Holland, *Herwologia Anglica* (1620), facing p. 88; reproduced courtesy Folger Shakespeare Library, Washington, D.C.

the manner in which he always guarded his camps with sentinels. The unknown fate of the 1586 fifteen-man garrison, left by Grenville, illustrates the consequences likely to be met by scattered civilians in the uncivilized forest.

The total number of the 1585 expedition probably did not exceed six hundred men, three hundred being seamen necessary to man the ships. The other three hundred men served as soldiers and gunners and included the 108 men left on Roanoke Island as colonists and specialists. The areas from which the colonists were recruited appear to have been primarily the western counties of Devonshire and Cornwall, Middlesex, London, Oxford, Cambridge, and perhaps Wales. Many of the men were related by marriage or were living as close neighbors.

It is known, of course, that Ralegh and Grenville were both from the West Country and that Grenville actively recruited ships and personnel in that region after Ralegh's bill had been approved by the House of Commons. An altercation occurred between two boats on the Thames River, probably in February, 1585. The altercation involved "a double whery of foure oares" belonging to Ralegh, a "Captayne Hamades a gentleman of the said Sir Walter Rawleighes," and one John Stiles, a Thames waterman "hired by Sir Walter Rawleighe knighte to goe to the seas in his then appoynted viadge." Legal depositions taken as a result of this incident reveal that the Thames watermen were also a source of recruits for the venture. Indeed, Robert Holecroft, a member of this 1585 colony and possibly its lawyer, appeared in court representing some of these watermen after his return to England.

An additional source of recruits as colonists and crew members was from the ranks of impressed foreign seamen. The master of the *Waterhound* of Briell, Holland, for example, was imprisoned aboard ship for thirty weeks during the 1585 voyage. Depositions discovered in the Spanish Archives describe the experiences of two Spaniards—Pedro Diaz and Hernando Altamirano—both captured by Grenville during the 1585 expedition, as well

20

as those of Darby Glande, an Irishman, who after being impressed served as a member of the colony under Lane. Drafted for the approval of the queen (but never issued) was a commission giving Ralegh powers necessary for the impressment of such ships, soldiers, and sailors as he might deem necessary for his preparations.

Significantly, among the leadership of the expedition and the colony were four current or former members of Parliament (with a possible fifth in Lane himself); at least one knight, in the person of Grenville, and four other members destined to receive knighthood; two former sheriffs in either England or Ireland; one faculty member from an Oxford college; and four university graduates, three being from Oxford and one from Cambridge (plus two more who eventually would obtain degrees from Oxford). This gathering, complemented by Ralegh's own associations, previously discussed, certainly constituted a remarkable group of political, intellectual, and professional leaders for that day.

As to the various skills represented among the colonists, the Spanish prisoner Hernando Altamirano, captured on board a Spanish frigate in the Mona Passage during the outbound voyage, reported that the expedition included men trained in all trades. This statement, of course, does not reveal any explicit information concerning the men who remained as members of the colony. Lane mentioned a "Master Yougham," listed in the roster of colonists as Doughan Gannes and subsequently identified as the same Joachim Ganz known to have conducted metallurgical research in 1581 to find improved methods of smelting copper. As Lane's minerals expert in 1585, Ganz asserted that the Indians were able to melt copper, which was identified as one of their richest possessions, although it is now known that the Indians were never able to heat the ore sufficiently to smelt it. There was a physician with Lane as late as September 8, 1585, but he probably returned with Grenville; in addition, a surgeon may have been present in the person of Haunce Walters. Lane appears to have had the services of at least one apothecary, even though others may have returned to England with Grenville. There is the possibility that a lapidary was a member of the colony, as recommended in the Cavendish notes. If so, he was probably the person responsible for the gathering of some 5,000 pearls, which were apparently lost upon leaving Roanoke Island in 1586. There was no designated chaplain for the colony, although Harriot relates in his *briefe and true report* his own private efforts in ministering to the savages, his official duties being otherwise prescribed. The documents reveal that there were present men who were expert in the art of fortification as well as in the trades of brickmaker, carpenter, and thatcher. Evidently, few men possessed agricultural skills, but it appears that a shoemaker, a basketmaker, two lawyers, a customs official, and two noted mathematicians may well have been among the colonists.

Relatively few documents concerning the abortive 1585 supply squadron and the 1586 ventures are extant. The 1585 supply squadron was planned by Ralegh and designated to follow Grenville to Virginia, leaving England in June, 1585. Queen Elizabeth, however, diverted this supply expedition to Newfoundland with orders for the English fishing vessels there, forbidding them to sell their catches to the Spanish. As a secondary mission, the expedition was to seize all the Spanish shipping encountered. The venture was commanded by Bernard Drake, who was knighted by the queen upon his return from this highly successful excursion. George Raymond, who was captain of the *Lion* in Grenville's expedition of 1585, met Drake near Newfoundland and entered into a consortship with him to privateer in the Azores prior to their return to England. Whether this rendezvous was planned in advance or simply coincidental is not known, although the latter is more probable.

Apart from Bernard Drake, only the names of Amyas Preston and Robert Bragge survive as members of the 1585 supply expedition. Amyas Preston, principal victualler of Drake's ship, returned to England in charge of a prize taken on the way to Newfoundland. In 1586 Preston and the executors of the then deceased Bernard Drake instigated a libel suit in connection with the financial returns of the voyage. Robert Bragge, identified as a citizen and merchant of London, claimed to have been a member of the crew.

The 1586 ventures were carried out by a supply ship and a supply squadron, the latter commanded by Sir Richard Grenville. Nothing is known about the crew of the supply ship, although a vessel of its size would probably have carried a complement of from twenty to sixty men, depending upon whether it was outfitted as a warship or as a common merchant vessel. As to Grenville's group, several names are known, apart from his own. Carew Ralegh, Sir Walter's older brother, attempted to raise funds for the venture in Exeter, identifying himself with the preparations for the voyage. Martin White, who served as Ralegh's factor at Plymouth, was also involved. John and Arthur Facy, who were destined to take part in later voyages to Virginia, were both engaged, either as master and captain of one vessel or in similar positions aboard one of the prizes sent back to England. Arthur Facy did some privateering on his own account before his participation in John White's abortive 1588 venture.

Sir Richard Grenville arrived in Virginia with his expedition after Sir Francis Drake had already found Lane's colonists in dire circumstances and returned them to England. In order to hold the fort while awaiting Ralegh's supply ship and additional colonists, Grenville left fifteen men as a garrison. Among these fifteen were two men who were designated as being "in charge": a "Master Cofar," possibly Coffin, and one named Chapman. In 1587 White learned that one of these men had been ambushed by the Indians while speaking with them in a friendly parley. During the 1586 voyage Grenville also made use of Pedro Diaz, a Spanish pilot whom he had captured aboard the *Santa Maria de San Vicente* in 1585. A deposition made by Diaz lends some insight into the size and strength of the 1586 expedition, which Diaz described as consisting of six ships and four hundred sailors and soldiers provisioned for one year. Diaz was apparently confined by Grenville at Bideford, where, between voyages, he published a work concerning the training of pilots at Seville, Spain, for service in the West Indies.

The 1587 Colony and Related Expeditions

Governor John White left England in 1587 intending to plant his colony in the Chesapeake Bay area after stopping by Roanoke Island and probably resupplying Grenville's fifteen-man garrison. Finding little trace of the garrison and leaving the colony on Roanoke Island instead of on the Chesapeake Bay, White returned to England in early November of that year to obtain supplies for sustaining the settlement. The advent of the Spanish Armada's attack on England and its aftermath precluded his successful return to Roanoke Island until 1590. Although White did embark on an abortive voyage in 1588, it proved to be a bitter disappointment for him. His 1590 voyage resulted only in his learning that the 1587 colony had abandoned the Roanoke Island settlement. Since the location to which the 1587 colony moved has never been discovered, it has come to be known in history as the "Lost Colony." These three ventures relating to the Lost Colony constitute the second and last major effort by Ralegh and his associates to plant and sustain an English colony on American soil.

With the return to England of the 1586 expedition and the resulting discovery that Governor Lane and his colonists had already arrived there, all colonizing efforts had to be reorganized. Recruits for settlement had to be found, shipping raised, and supplies and equipment collected in much the same manner as had been done two years earlier. A more practical comprehension of the problems of colonization, as well as more detailed information about the environment of the general area in which the settlement was to be made, had been gained, however, through the experiences of the 1585 settlers.

The idea of a military colony, as proposed in the Cavendish notes of 1584 or 1585, was rejected in 1587. Military rule had come to be viewed as an ineffective form of government for a successful permanent colony or, perhaps, only as a necessary first step toward permanent colonization. A new group of people, including men, women, and children, was selected as colonists, and a civilian political organization was devised to ensure effective governance in the new settlement. John White was appointed governor of the colony, and twelve assistants—"Roger Baylye, Ananyas Darr, Christopher Cooper, John Sampson, Thomas Steeuens, William Fullwoodd, Roger Pratt, Dyonise Harvye, John Nicholls, George Howe, James Plat, and Symon Fardinando . . ."—were chosen as members of the council. An examination of the complete list of colonists, including those names just cited, reveals that three of the latter—Fullwoodd, Nicholls, and Plat—did not accompany the expedition to America. It has been suggested that these men may have remained in England to supervise and manage the raising of ships and supplies for the colony. George Howe was killed by the Indians prior to John White's return to England.

Simon Fernandes remains one of the most controversial characters in the Roanoke saga. A Portuguese pilot transplanted to England by the 1570s, he married there and entered the service of both Sir Humphrey Gilbert and Sir Francis Walsingham prior to becoming involved with Ralegh and the Roanoke voyages in 1585, by which time he had participated in several privateering and reconnaissance ventures. In 1587 he was identified as a "London Gentleman" when included in the list of the new assistants. Although he was named as a colonist by White, he did not remain in Virginia and had no intention of doing so. His preoccupation with privateering was well known to the colonists, who regarded him as "not sufficient" to the task of adequately representing their interests in raising additional supplies in England. Fernandes, for example, is cited by White as being responsible for refusing to take the 1587 colonists to the Chesapeake Bay as planned, forcing them instead, in his haste to put to sea and search for prizes, to remain on Roanoke Island. Faced with Fernandes's duplicity and realizing that no other assistants were willing to return to England, the colonists persuaded John White to make the journey and to act as their spokesman in securing needed supplies, regardless of the fact that he served as their governor at Roanoke Island.

The recruiting of personnel for the 1587 colony appears to have been carried out primarily in regions other than Devonshire and Cornwall, which had contributed so much toward the support of the earlier expeditions. Some of the colonists are known to have come from the London section, Essex, or Cambridgeshire or to have been associated with those areas. A deposition made by Pedro Diaz reveals that Grenville went to London and recruited people there for the settlement. White also appears to have been partly responsible for enlisting volunteers, inasmuch as he expressed the wish not to return to England for supplies for fear of invoking criticism for "leauing the action, and so many, whome he partly had procured through his perswasions, to leaue their natiue Countrey, and vndertake that voyage. . . ." Some colonists may have been recruited from Portsmouth and the surrounding area as well. White's expedition sailed from that port, stopping on the way to Virginia for eight days at Cowes on the Isle of Wight, just across the bay from Portsmouth. Sir George Carey, vice admiral of Hampshire and governor of the Isle of Wight, had his headquarters at Carisbrooke Castle, located only eight miles from Cowes.

Another area from which recruits may have been obtained was Ireland. There were at least two Irishmen—Darby Glande and Dennis Carroll—in the expedition when it left England, but both jumped ship in the West Indies and joined the Spanish. It is also thought that Thomas Butler and James Lasie may have been Irish or possibly Anglo-Irish. The presence of an Irish group among the colonists might indicate that White already had some connections in that country.

The Lost Colonists of 1587 were a totally different group of people from those who constituted the 1585 colony. As has been observed, women and children were included in this group, which had not been done previously. Apart from John White, only two of Lane's men—John Wright and James Lasie—returned to Roanoke Island as members of the new colony. The names of these two Lost Colonists are identical to those of two of Lane's men, although this circumstance is not conclusive proof that they were in fact the same persons. The earlier settlers became disaffected with the colonizing experiment, possibly because of their unpleasant experiences with the Indians, perhaps because of the absence of gold or other rich resources in Virginia, or perhaps because of the strict military discipline maintained by Lane over his men. Whatever the cause, it appears that some of these people, upon their return to England, conducted an adverse publicity campaign against the Virginia ventures.

The 1587 expedition was originally projected to establish a permanent settlement of 150 colonists, although White actually left only 114 members of the expedition plus two children born on Roanoke Island before his departure for England; he also returned to their people the two Indians—Manteo and Towaye—who had been taken to England previously. The thirty-six missing colonists may have been with Captain William Irish, who was conducting a privateering expedition in the West Indies for Sir George Carey and who, apparently by previous arrangement, was to call at the new settlement before returning to England. In the West Indies, Irish captured a Spanish sailor by the name of Alonso Ruiz, who later reported in a deposition to the Spanish authorities that he had been to the Bahia de Santa Maria, the Spanish name for Chesapeake Bay. This deposition suggests that Irish may have gone to the site originally contemplated for the new colony but, finding no trace of it, returned to England, presumably with the thirty-six additional colonists. Pedro Diaz reported in his deposition that 210 colonists, counting women and children, were prepared for the 1587 colony. Diaz's total was not exact, but he was correct in regard to the inclusion of women and children.

The list of 1587 colonists gives the names of 91 men, 17 women, and 11 children, including those of the two children born on Roanoke Island before White's return to England. Of the ninety-one men, there must be deducted the names of White and Fernandes, both of whom returned to England, and that of George Howe, who was killed by the Indians. The name of Thomas Harris is listed twice, which is very likely an oversight, although it is not inconceivable that two men with such a common name were both present.

The final count of the Lost Colonists actually totals 116, counting Thomas Harris twice. This figure can be divided into families, depending upon various speculative relationships. Of the 88 living men left by White, between 9 and 11 probably had their wives with them, two couples having one child each; and four other men probably had a young son, a younger brother, or some other young relative with them. This analysis of the number of colonists on Roanoke Island leaves between 73 and 75 men with no apparent attachments in the settlement, from 6 to 8 single women, and 3 children seemingly unrelated to any member of the colony. The apparently unattached women and children might possibly have been servants in some cases or stepchildren in others.

Research by historian William S. Powell into the personal backgrounds of the Roanoke voyagers indicates that among the 1587 colonists there appears to have been at least one former sheriff, one faculty member from a Cambridge college, one lawyer with a Bachelor of Civil Law degree from Oxford, a goldsmith, a husbandman, a tailor, 2 gentlemen other than those listed as assistants, and 2 men who had served prison terms for stealing. The christening of the Indian Manteo would suggest the presence of a clergyman, but since there was no indication that one remained with the settlers, it is possible that a chaplain aboard one of the ships performed the ritual. Hakluyt, in fact, observed in the dedication of his translation of René de Laudonnière's *L'histoire notable de la Floride* that Ralegh intended "to sende some good churchmen thither . . . ," implying that none had yet been sent to Virginia as colonists. With White's departure for England the 1587 colony passed into historical oblivion.

Prompted by the impending attack of the Spanish Armada in 1588, the English Privy Council ordered a stay of all shipping intending to clear for foreign ports. Although this stay order prevented a much larger expedition under Grenville from sailing to Roanoke, White was able to obtain permission to depart in 1588 with two pinnaces on a voyage for the relief of the colonists in Virginia. White wrote a brief narrative about his 1588 voyage but mentioned no names and gave no information concerning the personnel of the vessels. His only statement in this connection was that the two pinnaces carried fifteen planters for the colony. Pedro Diaz said that Grenville embarked on this expedition with seven men and four women for the settlement, but he may have mentioned only those passengers who were aboard the pinnace *Brave,* which he served as pilot. Diaz's statement suggests that Grenville may have had more to do with the preparations for this voyage than White had intimated. Diaz also mentioned Captain "Artefaz"—Arthur Facy, captain of the *Brave*—as being the same man who had been with Grenville in 1586. From White's narrative, it appears that Facy frequently had privateering on his mind, a tendency he had previously displayed in 1586; and White places the blame for the misfortune of the 1588 voyage squarely on Facy's shoulders by declaring: "God [was] justly punishing our former theeurie of our euil desposed mariners." These sentiments were similar to those expressed by White in 1587 concerning Fernandes's privateering.

The 1590 expedition was likewise planned upon a larger scale than that upon which it was actually undertaken. It was to have been made in conjunction with a privateering expedition of John Watts of London, with Watts's ships to carry White, additional settlers, and provisions for the colonists, in return for which Ralegh was to obtain a clearance order permitting the ships to sail. According to White, only at the last moment was he allowed to board Watts's ship, the *Hopewell,* and the other colonists were forced to remain in England. William Sanderson dispatched a ship of his own, the *Moonlight,* under Captain Edward Spicer, formerly the master of one of the 1587 vessels. Although there is no evidence to confirm this conjecture, it is thought that some stores and provisions for the Roanoke colonists may have been taken aboard the *Moonlight.* Captain Abraham Cocke commanded the *Hopewell,* which, together with Sanderson's *Moonlight,* did reach Hatarask[2] in Virginia, making White's brief search for the 1587 colonists feasible. Captain William Irish, who had visited the Chesapeake Bay in 1587, again commanded ships in 1590 and 1591, engaging in privateering in the West Indies. It is possible that there had been some agreement under which he was to call at the Roanoke settlement on his return to England, either in 1590 or 1591, as he had previously done in the Chesapeake region; however, no evidence to support this speculation has been discovered.

---

[2]Hatarask was the name given after 1585 to Port Ferdinando, which was located just north of present Oregon Inlet. Hatarask was also the name given the island to the south of that inlet.

III. Ships of the Expeditions

English Ships of the Elizabethan Era

Except for the acquisition of personnel, the most important effort involved in the preparations for an expedition such as that of 1585 was the procurement of the proper type and quantity of shipping required to meet the needs of the proposed colony. Compared to the gigantic supertankers of the present time, whose displacement reaches into the hundreds of thousands of tons, ships of the Elizabethan age, which might attain a burden of 1,100 tons, were like chips of wood upon the ocean.

The method of measuring the size of a ship in that time was much simpler than it is at the present time. Rather than computing the weight of the water displayed by the craft, one measured the weight of the cargo a vessel could carry. This calculation was performed by using one of two systems: tons "burden," meaning the tonnage of the light, bulky cargoes such as might be contained in barrels or cases; or "ton and tonnage," meaning the weight of heavy, compact cargoes such as coal or sand. The tons burden of the average ship of the period ran about 100 tons, and the burden for an average large

This painting by Darrell McClure shows a typical sixteenth-century English ship laboring through high seas.

vessel, fit to be the flagship of an important expedition, varied from 200 to 300 tons.

High aft structures, or sterncastles, were the dominant characteristic of a sixteenth-century ship, affording it some protection from the heavy seas through increased buoyancy. Guns were mounted on the main deck and below decks, wherever possible, and even in the quarters of the captain, crew, and passengers. The open deck area was never very spacious. The captain's and the master's quarters were located under the sterncastle, and the crew's berths were among the stores of ropes and tackle in the forecastle. The crew lived on the main deck among the guns and ship-handling equipment. Below this deck was a half deck where the petty officers had their quarters, and below this area was the hold, in which the powder, water, and provisions were stored and where the cookroom was located. The cookroom, where rations were prepared for all hands, was a solid and immovable brick structure, built at the bottom of the hold upon the ballast, which was usually gravel. Much refuse and waste seeped into this ballast, giving rise to unsanitary conditions, and fire, which sometimes emanated from the cookroom area, was a frequent source of disaster.

The crew for a large man-of-war of the British navy has been estimated at from one man for every 2 tons burden to three men for every 5 tons, the ratio for merchant ships being one man for every 5 tons. Of course, the smaller the ship, the larger the proportion of manpower to the tonnage. In warships, one third of the crew were soldiers, one seventh were gunners, and the rest were designated as mariners. In merchant vessels, which normally carried no soldiers, one twelfth of the crew were classified as gunners and the balance as seamen. Crew members included the captain, master pilot, boatswain, quartermaster, master gunner, surgeon (usually), yeomen of the sheets (who supervised the setting and adjusting of sails) and of powder, a drummer, a trumpeter, an armorer, all their respective mates and common seamen, and perhaps a steward or cabin boy for the use of the captain and master.

The smaller ships, called pinnaces, had flushed decks with no raised extremities fore and aft; they varied from minimum to as much as 50 tons burden. The larger pinnaces ranged from 20 to 50 tons and were often equipped with sails as a means of propulsion. The smaller pinnaces were either towed or carried by the larger ships, being in reality only ship's boats. In his *Discourse of Western Planting,* Richard Hakluyt suggested the use of ships, pinnaces, barks, and busses with flat bottoms, evidently because of the shallow sounds described by Arthur Barlowe in his newly received report.

Ships of the 1585 Expedition and Related Voyages

In 1584 Philip Amadas and Arthur Barlowe employed two vessels that the latter, in his discourse on the voyage, called "barks." Because Walter Ralegh's 200-ton *Bark Ralegh* had been recalled from Sir Humphrey Gilbert's disastrous 1583 expedition to Newfoundland, it has been suggested that Amadas used this vessel as his flagship. Barlowe most likely commanded a smaller vessel such as Ralegh's small 50-ton bark the *Dorothy,* which is known to have been used in the 1585 venture. In his narrative, Barlowe states at one point that upon arriving in Virginia members of his expedition manned their "boates" to the land, and at another point that they rowed their vessels to the land. These statements indicate that at least one of the ships was of sufficient size to carry or tow (or both) more than one small pinnace of some undetermined nature. Apart from these references, little else is known about the 1584 ships.

Much can be gleaned, however, from various documents with respect to the shipping of the 1585 expedition, and several references from Spanish records provide additional insight into Ralegh's preparations. Bernardino de Mendoza, Spanish ambassador to France, had previously been summarily expelled from England as Spanish ambassador for having been involved in a plot against the queen's life. He periodically reported to King Philip II of Spain on the progress of Sir Walter Ralegh's and Sir Francis Drake's plans concerning Florida, which, so far as Spain was concerned, included English Virginia and the West Indies. Mendoza had at least one personal agent operating in England, gathering such information, but, as Spanish agents in England were slowly apprehended, his reports gradually lost accuracy.

On April 18, 1585, just over one week after Grenville's fleet had set sail from Plymouth, Mendoza forwarded to Philip II a report that Ralegh had "five ships of 150 tons and eight pinnaces of 25 tons" being prepared at Plymouth. This statement would appear to be unreliable since only six to eight vessels of any description set sail, according to the various English accounts. However, this seemingly exaggerated estimate may reflect at least some additional preparation in the form of a larger complement of ships diverted at the last moment to Sir Francis Drake's fleet or retained to form a portion of the supply expedition that was to have set sail under Bernard Drake in June, 1585. In an earlier dispatch, Mendoza had also noted that

The Thames River, shown here as it appeared in the sixteenth century, was London's main highway to Old World trade and New World exploration. One of the busiest ports in the world, London on the Thames governed the growth of the British Empire. Portion of engraving by Cornelis Visscher; reproduced courtesy Folger Shakespeare Library.

Ralegh was having built four new pinnaces of 20 to 30 tons each and had bought from the Dutch two flyboats of 120 tons each and two 40-ton barks. Some of these vessels most likely formed a part of Grenville's fleet.

At least some of the shipping for the 1585 expedition was furnished and outfitted on the Thames, near Greenwich, although the degree to which this activity was conducted there is not certain. The incident, previously mentioned, that occurred in a boat on the Thames River and involved Philip Amadas and the Thames watermen points toward the probability that sizable maritime preparations were under way in the London area. This incident is especially significant since Elizabeth provided the ship used as the admiral of the expedition. And, as alluded to earlier, Grenville, following his participation in Parliament's consideration of Ralegh's bill, was in the West Country recruiting both personnel and shipping and joining the London detachment at Plymouth with at least one ship and possibly more.

The size of the seven ships that comprised Grenville's 1585 fleet ranged from a possible 20 tons to 160 tons burden. The largest of these ships was the *Tiger,* rated at about 160 tons, which served as the admiral of the expedition; the vessel was contributed by the crown from the Royal Navy lists.

The *Tiger* as originally built for Henry IV in 1546. From M. Oppenheim, *A History of the Administration of the Royal Navy and of Merchant Shipping in Relation to the Navy,* Volume I: *MDIX-MDCLX* (London and New York: John Lane, 1896), frontispiece.

The *Tiger* was originally built in 1546 for Henry VIII as an experimental galleass with oars near the waterline and a spar ram in the bow. It then carried only eight guns on a side, was built high off the water with a flat top deck, and carried the normal square-rigged sails of the day. This design apparently did not prove too successful, and in 1570, after a period of disuse, the *Tiger* appears to have been rebuilt. The ram and oar ports were removed, and more guns were added. Having a shorter-than-normal keel and fitted with a small one-deck-high cabin on the bow and a similar larger cabin on the stern, the *Tiger* looked quite different from conventional ships of the time.

Until recently this vessel was believed to have led the 1585 expedition; however, some evidence has been found to suggest that the Royal Navy's *Tiger*, perhaps because of its age and condition, was traded to Sir William Winter in 1583 or 1584 in exchange for his *Seadragon*. The two ships also exchanged names, which means that the 1585 *Tiger* would have been in reality the old *Seadragon*, and the *Seadragon*, which formed part of Sir Francis Drake's fleet in 1586, would probably have been the Royal Navy's old *Tiger*. This would also mean, coincidentally, that the new *Tiger* may have helped take Lane's colonists to Roanoke Island and that the old *Tiger* may have helped bring them home again in 1586 when Drake took the Lane colonists back to England.

This *Tiger-Seadragon* trade, if verified, would help to explain some of the discrepancies between what is known of the old *Tiger* and what records reveal about the 1585 *Tiger*. Mendoza's description to Philip II of a 180-ton vessel (somewhat less in English tons) fits closer to the 160 tons burden at which the *Tiger* is believed to have been rated in 1585. The exchange of the ships would also help to account for the difference between John White's drawing of the 1585 *Tiger* and what is known of the features of the old Royal Navy

John White's painting of what was probably the 1585 *Tiger* at Puerto Rico. From Paul Hulton and David Beers Quinn, *The American Drawings of John White, 1577-1590* (London: Trustees of the British Museum; Chapel Hill: University of North Carolina Press, 2 volumes, 1964), II, plate 2.

Tiger, as described above. The 1585 *Tiger* is shown by White to have had three masts, being square-rigged, and a spritsail on the bow to hold the vessel on course. It appears to have been designed very much like most common commercial vessels of that day. In fact, it has been suggested that the 1585 *Tiger* was very similar to the *Mayflower* of Pilgrim fame and was possibly built within a few years of the other ship. The *Mayflower* carried 108 people and utilized 1.6 tons of cargo space per passenger, whereas the 1585 *Tiger* carried 160 people and allotted .9 tons of cargo space per person. Under these conditions living space would certainly have been more crowded for

John White's painting of what most likely was the 1585 *Tiger* at Salinas Bay, Puerto Rico. From Hulton and Quinn, *The American Drawings of John White, II,* plate 3.

the Roanoke colonists than for the Pilgrims of some thirty years later. The 1590 Royal Navy list describes the 1585 *Tiger* as having a 64-foot length, a 23-foot beam amidships, a 50-foot keel length, and a 13-foot maximum hold depth below the lowest deck to the keel. It had two decks: a main or "orlop" deck that covered the hold, and a top deck.

The history of the 1585 *Tiger* after the Roanoke voyages is not as illustrious as that of the *Mayflower,* however. The *Tiger* never made another transatlantic crossing. After service under Grenville during the 1588 battle against the Spanish Armada, it remained on the active Navy list for some years. It was then converted into a "lighter," or barge, for ship-to-shore ferry service for some undetermined period of time before 1602, when it was given the task

The *Mayflower II,* a modern replica of the original seventeenth-century *Mayflower,* under sail. Photograph courtesy Plimoth Plantation, Inc., Plymouth, Massachusetts.

of carrying across the Medway River the great chain that protected the royal dockyards from intruders.

The *Tiger* is thought to have had its armament increased for the 1585 voyage and reportedly carried 6 demi-culverin, 10 sakers and 2 minions, 2 falcons, 4 fowlers, and 4 bases, together comprising a battery of 28 pieces of ordnance. (For a description of the relative size and range of this ordnance, see Appendix B.) John White's painting of the *Tiger* shows clearly that fourteen guns could be placed on each side of the ship. Historian David Beers Quinn believes that the armament could indeed have been increased over the usual numbers for this voyage, which would also account for the larger number of persons on board. Indeed, Mendoza reported earlier that the *Tiger* was armed with twelve cannon when received by Ralegh from the crown.

Concerning the other ships of the expedition, not as much of their history is known, for, inasmuch as they were private vessels and not ships of the Royal Navy, fewer records of previous owners have survived. The documents, however, give sufficient information to yield an understanding of their characteristics. The *Roebuck* was rated in the *Tiger*'s journal as a flyboat of 140 tons, and it was possibly one of the two flyboats reported by Mendoza as having been purchased by Ralegh from the Dutch. It has been described by historian Kenneth R. Andrews as having been probably "superior to any merchantman in design and armament, particularly because Ralegh strongly opposed the older fashion of high-charged ships." Ralegh's *Roebuck* also seems to have been involved in some privateering in the English Channel on April 9, 1585, when it took as prizes a French ship laden with linen and wheat and, probably, the *Waterhound* of Briell, with a cargo of wine. John Clarke was not only the *Roebuck*'s captain during these encounters but also served in the same capacity during the voyage to Virginia, when the ship was very likely designated as the vice admiral. The *Roebuck* later took part in the 1592 capture of the *Madre de Diós*, a 1,600-ton Portuguese carrack, for which Ralegh may have received some £6,000 in profit. The size of the *Roebuck,* and perhaps also that of the *Lion,* was sufficiently large to enable either vessel to tow a pinnace.

The *Lion,* or *Red Lion of Chichester,* rated at 100 tons and possibly being the other 120-ton Dutch flyboat mentioned by Bernardino de Mendoza, was the next most important vessel in the group. Its captain, George Raymond, met with Bernard Drake of the *Golden Royal* in the vicinity of Newfoundland on the return voyage of 1585 and entered into a consortship with him to conduct privateering operations in the Azores before continuing to England. Ralegh's ship of 1586 was of the same tonnage as the *Lion,* indicating that the latter might have made another trip to Virginia in that capacity during the year following the Grenville expedition. It might also have had, as suggested above, a pinnace in tow.

The two remaining vessels of the 1585 fleet, which could be called ships in their own right, were the *Dorothy* and the *Elizabeth,* both small barks of 50 tons. The former may have been commanded by Arthur Barlowe, although there is no evidence that he was with the voyage. The background of the *Dorothy* is not known, but it could have been one of the two 40-ton barks that Mendoza reported as having been purchased by Ralegh from the Dutch; actually, it was described simply as "a small barke" by the author of the *Tiger* journal. It is possible, furthermore, that the *Dorothy* was in the company of the *Lion* when the latter met and was entered into consortship with Drake and the *Golden Royal.* As to the *Elizabeth,* it is known that Thomas Cavendish, the high marshal of the expedition, served as its captain. Lane declared

The *Elizabeth II,* a replica of the 1585 *Elizabeth,* is here shown under full sail in the North Carolina sounds. Permanently berthed at Manteo on Roanoke Island, the vessel is open to visitors as the *Elizabeth II* State Historic Site. Photograph by Paul S. Marley.

35

in his reminiscences of the voyage that Cavendish "furnished out a ship wherein he went as captain."

An example of a generous complement of men and armament such as that carried by large pinnaces like the *Dorothy* or the *Elizabeth* was given in a deposition by Hugh Harding, master of the pinnace *Conclude,* a 30- to 50-ton vessel that sailed with the 1590 expedition. Harding described the crew of the *Conclude* as consisting of 18 men and one boy and noted that the vessel was armed with 2 double bases, 5 or 6 harquebuses, one large-caliber harquebus called a "crocke," and about 10 muskets and calivers for hand-to-hand combat.

Concerning the smaller boats, only scattered information can be found. There were two small pinnaces, one being towed behind the *Tiger* and the other behind either the *Roebuck* or the *Lion.* The *Tiger* lost its boat during a storm in the "Bay of Portingal" and, while the expedition en route to Virginia was replenishing its supplies at its temporary fortifications at Guayanilla Bay, Puerto Rico, a replacement pinnace for the *Tiger* was constructed, launched, and rigged within ten days. These vessels of 20 to 30 tons were probably undecked and could be carried on board the larger ships if desired.

The new pinnace was used by Ralph Lane and his men while they accompanied Sir Richard Grenville in his exploration of Pamlico Sound after their arrival at Wococon Inlet, which was located about ten miles south of the present Ocracoke Inlet. Philip Amadas also used one of the pinnaces for an exploratory voyage in Albemarle Sound during the summer of 1585, prior to Grenville's embarkation for England. The record reveals that after Grenville's departure Lane utilized a pinnace left for him by Grenville to explore the upper reaches of that same body of water. Probably leaving this vessel anchored in the sound, Lane employed smaller boats to explore the Roanoke and Chowan rivers. Referring to those occasions when the pinnace was used, Lane complained that it was unsuitable for service in the shallow sounds, not only because it drew too great a displacement of water but also because it would not respond properly to oars. This last comment has led David Beers Quinn to suspect that Grenville had left Lane the pinnace recently built in Puerto Rico and that the vessel might well have been constructed too sturdily to possess satisfactory handling characteristics.

Cited in the documents are five different names applied to the small boats used by the expedition and the colony: a double-oared wherry, a tilt boat, a light horseman, a shallop, and a pinnace. The first mention of a "double whery of foure oares belonginge to Sir Walter Rawleighe" was in connection with the Thames incident; the reference is to the boat in which Philip Amadas was riding. Depositions given in the ensuing court case describe the vessel variously as a longboat and pinnace with a steersman, a helm and a rudder, and four oars. Lane recalled in his narrative that he had only one boat with four oars, which accommodated fifteen men with their "furniture, baggage and victuall for seuen dayes."

The tilt boat was mentioned but once and, on that occasion, as the vessel used by Grenville in his exploration of Pamlico Sound. Quinn also observes that this type of boat was employed on the Thames with an awning over the bow in order to protect passengers from the weather. He intimates, however, that this particular boat might well have been the same as the double-oared wherry referred to above, perhaps rigged with an awning.

The light horseman is first cited in conjunction with Lane's ascent of the Roanoke River. On this journey it is known that a light horseman was taken, along with the double-oared wherry. Lane had written earlier of planning this venture with two double-oared wherries, although he had but one, as well as the light horseman. The latter boat differed from the wherry with respect to design and capacity. It was lighter and longer than a wherry and was capable of being stored in sections on shipboard. Lane reserved the light horseman for himself at Roanoke Island in 1586, after he dispatched Prideaux with the pinnace to Hatarask Island, near old Port Ferdinando, and Captain Edward Stafford to the area of present Cape Hatteras. Prideaux's and Stafford's orders were not only to watch for the expected relief ships but also to feed themselves during those last days of the first colony in Virginia, when food was so scarce.

The shallop was larger than the normal ship's boat and was capable of being kept on board larger vessels; it was used on one occasion by some of the lesser members of Grenville's party while exploring Pamlico Sound. The term "pinnace" seems to have been loosely applied to any large boat in which fifteen or more men could be transported and which could make a limited voyage from a permanent base of operations. Effectively, it ranged anywhere from 15 to 30 tons in size. It was a required piece of equipment in privateering activities and was utilized to board prizes; and it was, of course, essential for exploratory ventures within the shallow waters of the Virginia sounds. During Grenville's return voyage in August, 1585, when he captured the *Santa Maria de San Vicente,* he evidently did not have small boats of any kind with him, having apparently left them with Lane, and he was forced to fashion one out of planks from boxes in order to board his prize. The *Tiger* journal states that the hastily built craft "sunke at the shippes side, as soone as euer hee and his men were out of it."

The abortive 1585 expedition, as it was finally organized under Bernard Drake, was led by the *Golden Royal* of Topsham, a vessel of 110 tons that "consorted with other ships," details about which are not known. Drake was ordered to proceed first to Newfoundland to instruct the English fishermen in that region not to take their catch to Spain, and then to seize as much Spanish shipping as possible. The *Job,* one of Ralegh's ships, rated at 70 tons and carrying a 16-ton load of "cedar wodde," met Drake when he was returning to England. The indication is that the *Job* was a part of the Drake expedition, although there is no direct evidence that it had departed England in company with the *Golden Royal.* It is possible that the wood had come from the Virginia colony and had been transshipped from the *Lion* when Drake met it off Newfoundland.

In 1586 two expeditions left England, the first being Ralegh's supply ship and the second being Grenville's reinforcement fleet for the colony. The supply ship was a 100-ton vessel that may have been the *Lion* of the 1585 venture. Apart from this possibility, nothing else is known about the ship itself. Grenville's squadron was comprised of at least two large ships and perhaps four or five smaller vessels. Pedro Diaz, who was the pilot of the *Santa Maria de San Vicente,* captured by Grenville in 1585, reported that the squadron consisted of six ships, one of 150 tons and the others ranging from 60 to 100 tons. On the other hand, Peter Godbecin, taken by Grenville from the *Angel* of Topsham during the outbound voyage of 1586, gave the number of ships as seven. Diaz further estimated the strength of the expedition at 400 sailors and soldiers. The preparations appear to have been conducted at both Bideford and Plymouth. Quinn suggests that the two larger ships, described as a flyboat and a frigate, may have been the *Roebuck* and the Spanish frigate captured in the Mona Passage of the West Indies during the outbound voyage of the 1585 expedition. There are relatively few surviving documents relating to the 1586 venture, whereas more extensive records are available concerning the expedition of the previous year.

Ships of the 1587 Expedition and Related Voyages

The 1587 expedition was not as extensive as that which deposited the Lane colony only two years earlier. It was apparently comprised of only two large seagoing vessels and a small pinnace with an unknown number of ships' boats. The larger ship, the admiral or flagship, was identified by John White as the *Lion.* It is likely that it was the same *Lion* that was used by Grenville in 1585, although there is no certainty, since the name was a common one among ships of that period. The 1587 *Lion* was of 120 tons burden and carried White as captain and Simon Fernandes as master. The 1585 *Lion* was listed as 100 tons. On his homeward voyage White traveled aboard the other of the two large vessels and stated in his narrative that the admiral had returned to Plymouth three weeks before his arrival, adding that it had taken no prizes and that its men had been stricken by sickness and death. There is evidence, however, that the crew of the *Lion* was mutinous in 1587 and that they "declared that weakness and feebleness that they had fallen into" was a result of their "spare and bad diet."

The other large ship is described simply as a flyboat. Its master was Edward Spicer, although nothing else is known concerning its size or its captain. Quinn suggests that a flyboat would have been at least of 100 tons burden, judging from the *Roebuck* of the 1585 expedition, which was listed as being 140 tons. White reported that upon weighing anchor for the return voyage from Virginia to England, twelve of the fifteen seamen on board were injured in an accident at the capstan. This number seems to have been an

This painting by Darrell McClure depicts some English crewmen watching a dangerous maneuver—a pinnace under sail passing through an inlet in treacherous currents.

unusually small complement to handle a vessel of that size, even though the officers should be added to this total.

The pinnace, commanded by Captain Edward Stafford, was left with the colonists. It was employed by White in crossing the sound from Port Ferdinando to Roanoke Island and must, therefore, have been small enough to have crossed the bar and to have sailed the shallow sound waters. Stafford also used the pinnace to sail from Roanoke Island to Croatoan on July 30, 1587, prior to White's departure. In 1590 White checked the cove near the settlement to determine whether or not he could find the pinnace and the boats, which he had left with the colony three years earlier. The fact that White found "foure yron fowlers" and various chests of equipment in 1590 may indicate that the Lost Colonists may not have had adequate means of water transportation to carry them to their new destination.

Sir George Carey had three ships privateering in the West Indies in 1587 under Captain William Irish; the vessels evidently were utilized in an attempt to make contact with the new settlement, which was to have been located on the Chesapeake Bay. Carey's ships included the *Commander* of 200 tons and 100 men, the *Swallow* of 70 tons and 40 men, and the *Gabriel* of 30 tons and 25 men; all were victualed for six months. Each of these vessels, described as a ship, a bark, and a pinnace in respective order, was issued a letter of reprisal authorizing it to conduct privateering operations at sea.

The two vessels used by White in 1588 were pinnaces—the *Brave* of 30 tons and the *Roe* of 25 tons. Although White referred to it as a bark on one occasion, the *Brave* is likely to have been the same ship as that captured by Grenville in 1586. White, along with Pedro Diaz, was aboard the *Brave*, which was captured and stripped of its cargo. It was barely able to return to England, as did the *Roe* a few weeks later. Nothing is known of the background of the *Roe*.

The 1590 ships were organized into three main groups. The largest contingent consisted of three ships owned by John Watts, which embarked on March 20, 1590, along with two shallops that sank after being towed for five days. The *Hopewell*, or *Harry and John*, of 140 to 160 tons, was the admiral, with Abraham Cocke serving as captain and Robert Hutton as master. It carried a complement of 40 to 80 men and 16 to 24 guns. The next largest ship was the 100- to 120-ton *John*, or *Little John*, which carried a possible 100 men and 19 guns and served as vice admiral of the squadron. Christopher Newport, later involved with the Jamestown settlement, was its captain and Michael Geare its master. The last vessel was the pinnace *John Evangelist*, with William Lane serving as captain. Nothing is known of its size or complement.

A second group of two ships put to sea with the intentions of calling at the Virginia settlement. One was the *Bark Young*, under the command of Captain William Irish, who was involved in the 1587 expeditions, and the other was the *Falcon's Flight*. The first vessel was owned by Sir George Carey and his associates, the latter by John Norris of Barnstaple, a subscriber to Grenville's 1586 voyage. These vessels were likely to have left before the

This painting by Darrell McClure depicts the drowning of Captain Edward Spicer when his boat overturned as it passed through Hatorask Inlet in 1590—the same voyage during which John White discovered that the 1587 colony was no longer on Roanoke Island.

other ships of the expedition, and they appear to have cleared port without a license to operate in foreign waters.

The last group of vessels set sail after the other ships had departed, Watts's privateers not being willing to wait for them to be equipped for sea duty. It should be remembered, however, that the second and third groups of ships were independent ventures. William Sanderson outfitted an 80-ton vessel, the *Moonlight,* or *Mary Terlanye,* with 40 men and 7 guns; the ship was commanded by Captain Edward Spicer, who was drowned while entering Hatorask inlet. It appears that this vessel was entered into a consortship with the *Conclude,* a 30- to 50-ton pinnace owned by Thomas Middleton and his associates, the verbal agreement to remain in force only until such time as Spicer could join Watts's ships. The *Conclude* was reported by Hugh Harding, its master, as being armed with 2 falcons, 2 double bases, 5 or 6 harquebuses, a large-caliber harquebus, and about 10 muskets and calivers for hand-to-hand fighting. Harding listed the *Conclude's* complement at eighteen men and one boy.

IV. Victualing and Supplies

Preparations for a colonizing effort required not only adequate provisions to sustain crew members on a round trip and colonists en route to their destination but also sufficient supplies to etablish and maintain the settlers until they could become self-supporting. Such an outlay included not only food and drink but also clothing, tools, weapons and ammunition, livestock and seed, printed books containing useful information, instruments for scientific observation and surveying, and such general furnishings and utensils as a household might require. The task of organizing such a settlement as was contemplated in 1585 imposed a coordinated effort on the part of a sizable group of people to mobilize a great quantity and variety of materials.

Food, or Victuals

The food and drink provisions were usually furnished by victuallers, who customarily retained, along with a crew and a ship's owners, a one-third interest in a vessel's share of any profits. Food rations aboard ship were not normally of superior quality. A month was counted as consisting of 28 days, 10 of which were designated as fish days and 16 as meat days, with four Fridays set aside as half-ration days, thereby saving two full days' ration per month. Typical fish-day fare included one pound of biscuit, one gallon of beer, one quarter of a stockfish (codfish) or one eighth of a ling (codfish family), one quarter pound of cheese, and one half pound of butter. A meat day provided the same rations as the above list, except that two pounds of salt meat, either beef or pork, were substituted for the fish. Sundays, Mondays, Tuesdays, and Thursdays were designated as meat days, while Wednesdays, Fridays, and Saturdays were observed as fish days. In addition to this schedule of distribution of individual rations, each man received one pound of bacon and one pint of peas per week. In victualing the expedition of 1584 and those subsequent to it, Sir Walter Ralegh's victuallers were obliged to compute in a similar manner the supplies that would be required.

Supplies

Among the ships' stores, which had to be furnished by the owners or the victuallers, if the two parties were not the same, were, among additional items, supplies such as bolts of canvas, cordage, masts and spars, anchors, cables and hawsers, repair timbers, pitch and tar, flags and pennants, oil, nails, and iron for mending ordnance. Most of these supplies were consumable, liable to breakage or loss, or otherwise susceptible to the hazards of the seas.

An estimate of the supplies and provisions that would be required for the settlers had to be based on such available sources as the report of Philip Amadas and Arthur Barlowe, the narratives of colonists from other nations (such as the French Laudonnière settlers), available Spanish writings, and the suggestions of individuals who had knowledge of privateering voyages and were familiar with the geography and resources of the New World. A sizable number of recommended items were listed by Richard Hakluyt, clergyman, in his *Discourse of Western Planting* and by his elder cousin, Richard Hakluyt, lawyer, in his "Inducements to the liking of the voyage intended towards Virginia." There is also an interesting list of equipment and supplies that the Spanish, in 1600, deemed necessary requirements for a successful campaign to attack and eliminate the English colony that they supposed still existed in the wilds of Virginia.

The 1585 Expedition and Related Voyages

The 1584 ships of Amadas and Barlowe were outfitted on the Thames and then dispatched to the "west of England," probably Plymouth, whence they embarked. The vessels were undoubtedly victualed and supplied in the same manner as any normal expedition designed for the conduct of exploratory or privateering activities, the only exception possibly being the inclusion of barter goods for trade with the Indians. The length of the Amadas and Barlowe venture was projected at slightly less than five months, from April 27 to mid-September, 1584, indicating that the members of the expedition were apparently prepared for a voyage of six months' duration, an extensive undertaking for that day. Among the goods included for trade with the Indians were hatchets, axes, knives, tin dishes, kettles, shirts, hats, and "some other thinges." The items of clothing were probably personal belongings traded on the spur of the moment, but the cutlery was likely brought for the intended purpose of barter. Barlowe stated that even though the Indians offered the Englishmen good exchange value for "their swords," they would not part with them, implying that they had been persuaded to trade other items of their personal effects that they could spare. Pots and pans were considered by the elder Hakluyt to have been excellent barter merchandise.

In December, 1584, Sir Richard Grenville assumed the task of preparing for the main colonizing expedition the following spring. The ships that had been requisitioned in London or in the West Country were also provisioned in those same locations. The queen's ship, the *Tiger,* and some of the other vessels were most assuredly on the Thames undergoing preparations in the early weeks of 1585, although they are not identified by name. Circumstantial evidence would indicate that Elizabeth may have granted Ralegh some supplies from the royal arsenal that were being delivered at the time of

Amadas's experience with the watermen on the Thames. Grenville, after provisioning his ships at Bideford, kept a rendezvous with Amadas on April 9, 1585, at Plymouth, the port from which they sailed.

It was undoubtedly agreed that some of the provisions for the colony were to be acquired in the Spanish West Indies, although the basic food supplies were likely brought from England. When the *Tiger* was nearly sunk on a sandbar at Wococon Inlet, south of present-day Ocracoke, most of its provisions, including wheat, rice, meal, and biscuit, were lost or damaged beyond use. Some rice, barley, and peas survived, perhaps aboard another vessel. The importance of these commodities, destined for the sustenance of the English colony, is sufficiently confirmed by the prompt dispatch to England of a ship, probably a prize, under the command of John Arundell, Grenville's half brother, to prepare additional supplies, including munitions, that Grenville could bring back to Virginia immediately upon his arrival in England. In his narrative, Lane lamented that the situation would have been far better for the colony if its members could have had the benefit of the supplies that had been initially prepared for them. This was certainly a reversal of his earlier opinion, written in a letter to Sir Francis Walsingham from Port Ferdinando prior to Grenville's departure for England in August, 1585, in which he expressed the belief that the colonists could support themselves upon the native products of the area.

While proceeding to Virginia, Ralegh's ships made numerous calls at various islands in the West Indies in order to obtain fresh water and victuals for the colonists and to trade with the Spanish for livestock, seed, and plants with which to equip the Virginia settlement. At Guayanilla, Puerto Rico, Grenville purchased a variety of animals, including hogs, sows, young cattle, and horses; some foodstuffs such as bananas and other fruit; and plants, including sugarcane. During a brief sojourn at Isabela, Hispaniola, he likely acquired horses with saddles and bits, along with cows, bulls, sheep, and swine. Some of the sugarcane, hides, pearls, ginger, and tobacco procured at Isabela might have been for the colonists, but most of this cargo was probably intended to be taken to England for sale in order to help defray the expenses of the venture. Bananas and other fruit were also gathered at Isabela. Grenville dispatched Lane to Salinas Bay, Puerto Rico, where he obtained a sizable quantity of salt, some of which may have been spoiled when the *Tiger* ran aground at Wococon Inlet and was very nearly lost. Another effort to gather salt for the colony at the nearby Caicos Islands in the Bahamas proved futile.

Several other landings were made, but there is no record of any acquisition intended for colonial provisions. In 1587 Simon Fernandes spoke of his friend, Alanson, from whom he would seek help at Isabela in obtaining supplies; this contact was probably established during the 1585 expedition and implies associations with merchants of the West Indies, of which no record has been found. Historian David Beers Quinn affirms that the French merchants "had a substantial hold on the illegal trade of this coast"; but by 1587

John White's drawing of the Salinas Bay entrenchments, which were built during the time salt was being gathered in Puerto Rico. Reproduced courtesy trustees of the British Museum.

Philip II ordered them to be removed from Hispaniola, although their removal proved to be only temporary.

Concerning the plants and animals proposed for use by the colonists in Virginia, there is found a helpful list of suggestions, once more in the writings of the two Richard Hakluyts. But a major fact unknown to Amadas and Barlowe, or to Lane and Grenville, was that Roanoke Island and the neighboring area were not suitable for stock raising. Only the milk cow, the hog, and some of the smaller fowl would have proved to be of any practical value to them.

In addition to the foregoing evidence that livestock was obtained by the English in the West Indies, there are some entries on this subject recorded in the Spanish documents. Pedro Diaz stated in his deposition that the English not only bartered for cattle, horses, and hogs but also landed these animals with the colonists. Alonso Ruiz, the Spanish seaman taken prisoner by Captain William Irish in 1587, reported that he had seen "traces of cattle and a branded mule" in the Chesapeake Bay region. This sighting probably occurred before John White arrived at Port Ferdinando with the 1587 colony on the first of August. Quinn further suggests that if these animals were indeed seen that far north, they were in all likelihood remnants of Lane's Chesapeake Bay expedition. Lane does indicate that the colony did possess mastiffs. These powerful dogs had been characterized by Richard Hakluyt, the clergyman, in his *Discourse of Western Planting* as being desirable "to kill heavie beasts of ravyne and for nighte watches." Lane mentions them as having been eaten as emergency victuals during one of the inland excursions by being made into a porridge mixed with sassafras leaves.

In his report to Ralegh, Arthur Barlowe listed numerous vegetables and fruits grown and used by the Indians for food; among these edibles were corn, nuts, melons and gourds, beans, peas, and grapes. This listing probably contributed to Lane's optimistic attitude concerning "living off of the land." The plants obtained by Grenville in the West Indies have already been mentioned, but what became of these acquisitions? Thomas Harriot gave a bleak picture in his *briefe and true report.* He said that the sugarcane perished because it was too late in the year for successful planting, and it was not very well preserved on board ship. He also added that oranges and lemons suffered a similar fate. Since the latitude of Roanoke Island was the same as that of other regions where these crops were successfully grown, Harriot assumed that these same plants would grow there as well, a fallacy likewise accepted by both Hakluyts. Harriot states that the experiments in the cultivation of barley, oats, and peas were successful, but the wheat they had procured was spoiled by salt water aboard ship. Of rye they had brought none. Most of the plants and cuttings, which they had taken great pains to keep alive during the voyage from the West Indies, either wilted or died.

Much was learned from the trading experiences of Amadas and Barlowe, leading to inclusion in the 1585 expedition of some interesting items for barter with the Indians. Prior to his departure for England in late August, 1585, Grenville probably conducted a rather active trade with the Indians in order to carry home with him as wide a range of native products as possible. Lane, on the other hand, was supported by both the younger Hakluyt and Thomas Harriot in his view that commerce could be at best only a minor activity and subsidiary asset to the colony. Trading did take place, however, and was probably directed by Thomas Harvey, a London citizen and member of the Grocers' Company, who served as chief merchant for the colony.

One of the commodities in most demand by the Indians was copper, a metal they highly prized. A large quantity of copper must have been brought by the colonists, since as late as March, 1586, Lane had apparently met the needs of the unfriendly Indians for the metal and still had some left, which he was unable to barter for corn. Lane's enemy, Pemisapan, chief of the Roanoke Indians, in turn bartered the copper he had thus acquired to win support among other Indian tribes for his schemes to annihilate the English. Harriot, who appears to have written the text for Theodor de Bry concerning this voyage, stated that glasses (probably mirrors or perhaps sandglasses), knives, and baby dolls were exchanged. In John White's drawing of a "Woman and Child of Pomeiooc," an Indian girl holds a small doll dressed in English clothes. De Bry's engraving of this scene features a rather expensive baby rattle of European origin in the Indian girl's other hand. The doll itself was more elaborate than the one depicted by White. Lane also observed that the Indians were very desirous of having clothes such as the English wore and that they particularly relished the coarser materials such as canvas, thereby implying that such materials were bartered.

The 1585 voyage of Bernard Drake to Newfoundland was intended as a supply expedition to Virginia but was diverted to Newfoundland and became a privateering venture. Other than the fact that Drake's *Golden Royal* was apparently being provisioned at Exmouth soon after Grenville's departure for Virginia, little else is known of this expedition's supplies. When the queen diverted Drake to Newfoundland, the nature of the supplies may well have been changed, at least to some extent, depending upon the amount of time available prior to sailing. The 1586 voyages, however, did sail as specially designed supply and reinforcement convoys prepared for the relief of the colony. It would be most enlightening if an inventory of the provisions and supplies of those expeditions had survived. In his *principall navigations voiages and discouries of the English nation* (1589), the sole source to include mention of Ralegh's supply ship, Richard Hakluyt, the clergyman, merely states that the vessel was "fraighted with all maner of things in most plentiful maner for the supplie and relief" of the colony. It may even have carried some of the armament and munitions that John Arundell had been dispatched to acquire in England at the same time he was assembling the necessary foodstuffs. It is certain, however, that Grenville did carry some ordnance for the colonists in 1586.

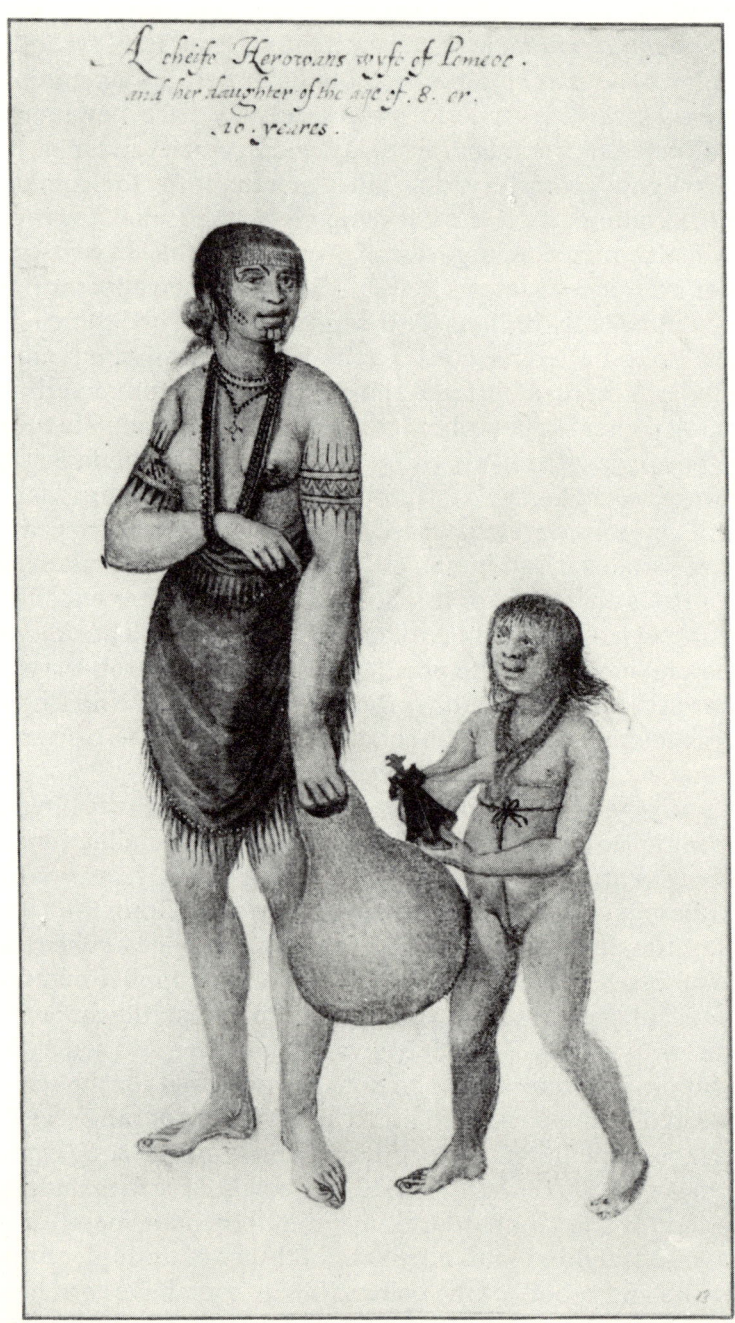

A cheife Heroroans wyf: of Pomeoc.
and her daughter of the age of .8. or.
.10 .yeares .

John White's drawing of an Indian woman and child, showing an English doll probably obtained through trade with the Lane colonists. Reproduced courtesy trustees of the British Museum.

As to Grenville's 1586 expedition, Diaz states that he left England fully provisioned for one year and that the men whom he left in Virginia as a garrison were likewise supplied for twelve months. Hakluyt, on the other hand, said that the latter group was equipped for two years. This convoy appears to have been prepared in Devonshire inasmuch as Ralegh's half brother, Carew, was attempting to raise support for it in Exeter, and Grenville was at Bideford preparing for its departure. At Southampton, in Hampshire, some of Ralegh's agents seized about 65 tons of wine from a French ship in the harbor, 21 tons of which were taken by Martin White, Ralegh's factor in Plymouth, for the provisioning of Grenville's 1586 vessels.

The 1587 Expedition and Related Voyages

The victualing and provisioning of the ships for the 1587 colony was probably conducted at Portsmouth, the port of departure. As has been observed, personnel were recruited in the London area. It is possible, however, that some of the shipping was prepared on the Thames and moved to Plymouth for final departure. Although there is no mention of support having been raised on the west coast around Bideford, White made a two-day stop at Plymouth after his eight-day sojourn at Cowes on the Isle of Wight. This Plymouth visit was probably for the purpose of receiving instructions, which were personally delivered to White's party by Ralegh, and to replenish the ships' supplies of food and water.

White evidently planned to obtain some stores for the colony while passing through the West Indies, probably in the same manner as had been done in 1585. In this regard, however, the sojourners of 1587 were not as successful as the earlier expedition had been. Simon Fernandes intended to stop at Isabela, Puerto Rico, and obtain the assistance of his friend Alanson in acquiring cattle, fruit, and plants, but he bypassed the port after apparently receiving word somehow that Alanson was no longer there. This attempt to gather supplies was thwarted after a similar opportunity to gather oranges, pineapples, and other fruit at San Germans Bay, Puerto Rico, had already been rejected in view of the presumably better possibilities at Isabela. White reported in his narrative of the 1587 voyage that Captain Edward Stafford was dispatched to the island of Vieques, located between St. Croix and Puerto Rico, for the purpose of obtaining sheep, but he gave no indication of Stafford's success. While at the Caicos Islands, White and his party were disappointed in not obtaining any salt, especially since they had been previously unsuccessful in eastern Puerto Rico. They "caught" many fowl and swans, but White does not indicate whether they took any wild game as stock for the Virginia colony.

Before leaving England, the ships were provisioned with foodstuffs and shipboard equipment in the same manner that the 1585 expedition had been prepared, with only the quantities varying because of the smaller size of the 1587 fleet. The stores taken as supplies for the colony would also have been on the same order. There was no mention that livestock was brought to Virginia by the 1587 colony, although Thomas Harriot intimated in his *briefe and true report* that various "Englishe sortes of cattaile" had been transported with the expedition and remained with the colony, an apparent reference to the cattle taken to Roanoke Island in 1585 that might have survived in the settlement area until 1587. That there was still some livestock alive in 1587 seems assured by the testimony of Alonso Ruiz, who apparently observed "traces of cattle and a branded mule"; but it is not known whether Ruiz saw the livestock in the Chesapeake Bay area or on the Carolina Outer Banks near Roanoke Island. In addition, White makes no mention in his narrative that seed was taken to the colony for planting, although it is quite safe to assume that the information, gathered from Harriot's studies and from the experiences of Lane's men in providing food for themselves in 1585, was put to practical use.

Of the 1588 voyage, it is known only that the vessels left Bideford on April 22 carrying biscuit, meal, and vegetables as provisions for the settlers, along with fifteen additional colonists "and all their provision." What was to have been included in the larger abortive expedition under Grenville is not known. On the basis of statements in the deposition of Pedro Diaz and the narrative of White, it is reasonably certain that both Grenville and White were active at Bideford in the preparations for the White expedition, which did sail.

The ships of John Watts, in 1590, were equipped on the Thames and taken to Plymouth, where they cleared for the West Indies. A general stay-of-shipping order prevented their departure, as had originally been planned, and White said that it was through his intercession that a license was procured. He claimed that he had discovered the plight of Watts's vessels and got Ralegh to obtain the queen's permission for their departure in return for the assurance, guaranteed by a £3,000 bond from Watts, that his ships would take some planters and supplies to the colony in Virginia. William Sanderson, on the other hand, implied that the license was granted to Watts and to himself.

Whichever was the case, Sanderson decided to send a ship of his own along with those of Watts; the latter, however, did not wait for Sanderson to outfit a vessel. By the time Sanderson had prepared his *Moonlight* and it had arrived at Plymouth, the *Hopewell* and its consorts had already departed for the West Indies. It is not certain to what degree the *Moonlight* was equipped on the Thames, since a number of its crew, including its master, John Bedford, were from Plymouth and the surrounding Devonshire area. At Plymouth, Captain Edward Spicer entered into consortship with the *Conclude* of that same port, where it was victualed for six to eight months. Hugh Harding, master of the *Conclude*, was also of Plymouth.

The *Moonlight* most likely carried stores and provisions for the Virginia colonists, since it is highly improbable that Sanderson would have sent a vessel to sea for any other reason. Sanderson claimed to have helped obtain a license for the *Moonlight* to clear port with the ships of Watts, the understanding apparently being that all the vessels would call by Virginia. There is an implication that Sanderson intended to send more than one ship but could not get others ready in time. In spite of John White's allegation that only he was allowed to board the *Hopewell,* it is David Beers Quinn's opinion that Abraham Cocke, captain of the vessel, might have refused the food and other light supplies White had assembled after a few pieces of ordnance had already been placed in the ship's hold. As to the two ships that sailed under William Irish, nothing is known of their preparation except the identity of their owners.

V. Ordnance and Related Materials

Ordnance in the Elizabethan period was undergoing a fundamental transformation. At the beginning of Elizabeth's reign in 1558 the longbow was the standard weapon in England; but by the time of Elizabeth's death in 1603 the musket and caliver had gained complete supremacy, although the bow was still employed well into the seventeenth century. Theoretically, if not in actual practice, the bow was considered "distinctly obsolescent" by 1588, with the pike, harquebus, and caliver being deemed the most forceful weaponry of a fighting unit. In 1552 the term "musket" was used to refer to a small breech-loading, swivel-mounted cannon, while by 1603 the musket was designated as a small arm or handgun that fired a 2- to 2½-ounce pellet and was used by infantrymen.

Shipboard armament, made of either brass or iron, ranged from the Cannon Royal, which weighed 8,000 pounds and threw a 60-pound ball, down to a 300-pound Robinet, which projected a one-half pound ball. The former had a maximum range of nearly two miles, while the latter could fire its missile nearly one mile. The Cannon Royal, or the full-size cannon, was rarely employed aboard ship, the 4,500-pound Culverin being among the largest that could be employed effectively (see Appendix B). In addition to heavy armament, a ship's arsenal usually included enough harquebuses (or

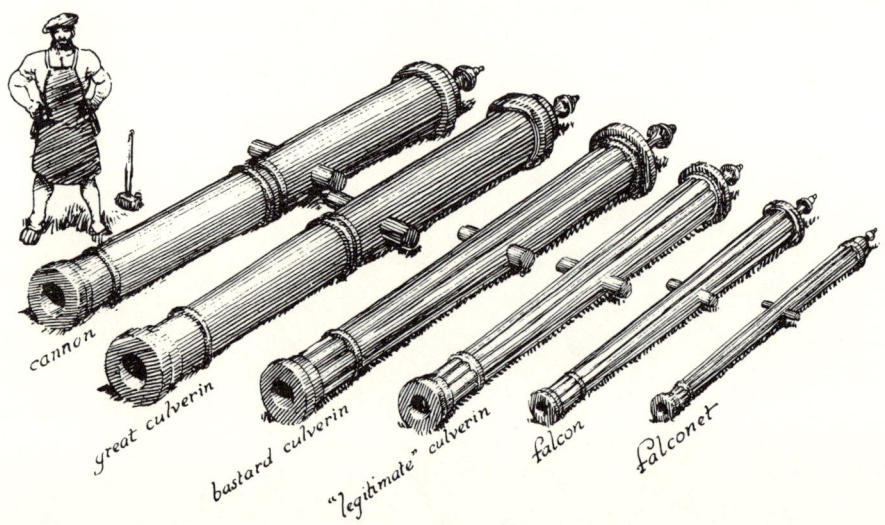

cannon *great culverin* *bastard culverin* *"legitimate" culverin* *falcon* *falconet*

Some varieties of sixteenth-century cannon. Illustration by Edwin Tunis. From Edwin Tunis, *Weapons: A Pictorial History* (Cleveland and New York: World Publishing Company, third printing, 1954), p. 89.

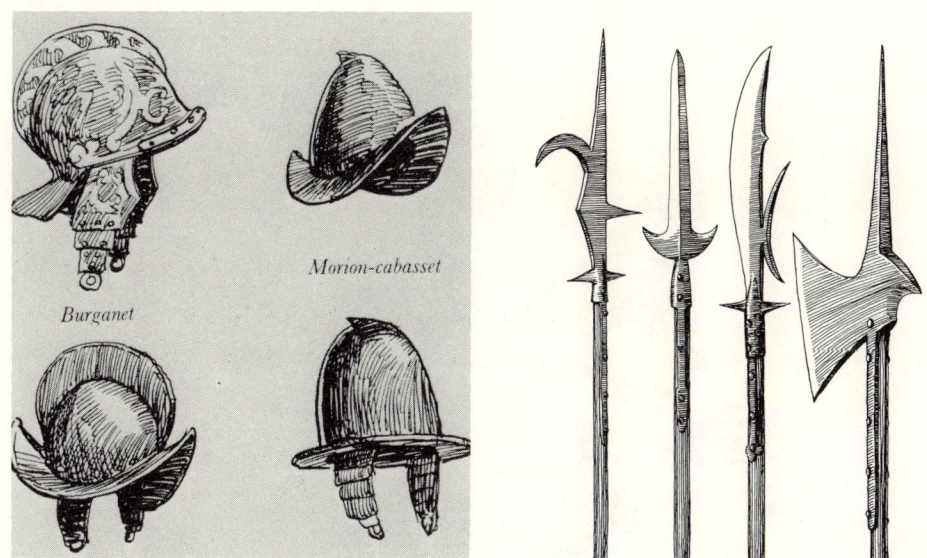

Typical sixteenth-century armored headgear and pole arms. Illustration by Edwin Tunis. From Tunis, *Weapons,* pp. 87, 85.

muskets), pikes, bills, corselets, and morions for the needs of each soldier aboard the vessel, with possibly a few extra weapons for replacements.

In the anonymous notes to Thomas Cavendish concerning the personnel of the Lane and Grenville expedition of 1585 were listed certain weapons and armor believed by its author to have been necessary for the colonists to possess in their struggle for survival against the Spanish and the Indians in the proposed settlement area. The use of armor was deemed necessary in the event the expedition ever had to fight the Spanish, but it was considered to be superfluous equipment for use against the Indians. The following specific weapons were recommended for acquisition: harquebuses, swords, halberds, bills, pikes, partisans, and battle axes as hand weapons, as well as the longbow.

Inasmuch as these small arms were the standard hand weapons of the time, they were undoubtedly furnished for the expedition, with each colonist probably being equipped with a minimum of one firearm and a hand weapon of some sort. Arthur Barlowe cited the employment of harquebuses in 1584, and Ralph Lane recorded the use of calivers against the Indians during the conspiracy of Pemisapan. John White illustrated both of these weapons in his drawings. Lane commented upon the use of a pistol, with which the "Colonel of the Chesepeans" wounded Pemisapan, as well as a "petronell," which was a heavy cavalry pistol carried in the belt and operated with either a wheel-lock, flintlock, or matchlock mechanism. In his narrative, Lane also made passing reference to targets, or shields. Thomas Harriot wrote of the colonists possessing "ordance great and small" that offered important military advantages over the Indians.

A harquebusier firing his weapon with a helper preparing ammunition. Illustration by Edward Tunis. From Tunis, *Weapons*, p. 78.

One of the most unusual weapons described by Harriot was what he called "wildfire woorkes." Historian David Beers Quinn observes that wildfire was a flammable compound, easily ignited, that had been used in warfare during the Middle Ages. Harriot probably had in mind this kind of fireworks, not the type used for entertainment and sometimes displayed at court for the amusement of the queen. In 1587 White received from the friendly Indians a report that a member of the second colony, left by Grenville in 1586, shot one of the hostile Indians with a wildfire arrow while they were attacking the settlement. This comment is the only reference indicating that the English actually used bows in Virginia, although they almost certainly used them in hunting. In this instance, the weapon was probably a bow employed for shooting arrows with some sort of incendiary device attached.

There is no doubt that some pieces of heavy artillery were provided for the bastions of the fort, which were constructed specifically for the purpose of harboring such weapons. Except for Harriot's remark concerning the "great" ordnance of the colony, no mention of the presence of such weapons is made in the 1585 documents; nonetheless, the archaeological reconstruction of Fort Raleigh gives some idea of number and location.

It is known that ordnance was to have been delivered to Lane's colony by the supply expedition of 1586, and during that year Grenville actually left four pieces of iron ordnance with the small colony of fifteen men whom he had left as a garrison at Lane's fort. These four iron fowlers were likely the ones seen by White in 1590, although he had made no mention of them in 1587. White also mentioned in 1590 that he had seen saker shot (for five-pounders) but could find no trace of the "last Falkons and small Ordinance which were left with them at my departure from them," meaning his departure in 1587. It is also established that in 1587 White provided "thirtie shotte, ten pikes, and ten targets" for the men assigned to man the pinnace and obtain salt at Puerto Rico, although he was dissuaded by Fernandes from seeking salt in that locality. Since these types of weapons are known to have been with the 1587 expedition, it is only reasonable to assume that the colony, too, was furnished with the same kinds of arms.

Pedro Diaz stated in his deposition that the men left by Grenville in 1586 were provided with four pieces of cast-iron artillery. In 1706-1708 John Lawson, North Carolina's surveyor general, who traveled widely throughout the colony, saw on Roanoke Island a cannon, which he described as a "small Quarterdeck Gun, made of Iron Staves and hooped with the same Metal." This may have been one of the original weapons of either the 1585, 1586, or 1587 colonies. In the same passage Lawson also referred to a brass gun and a powder horn, which likewise could have belonged to any one of the three colonies. The four iron guns cited by Diaz were undoubtedly those seen by White in 1590 when he returned for the last time to the site of the fort.

Within recent years a small iron cannonball was found about 1,100 feet east of the Fort Raleigh site. Archaeologists have speculated that the cannonball could be an Elizabethan falconet shot, although no proof of its age is available. The saker would probably have been the heaviest weapon the colonists could have transported from shipboard over the water and installed in the fort. The next-largest-sized weapon then in general use weighed approximately 3,000 pounds and would have posed a serious handling problem in small boats. The falconet, of course, could have been easily moved, since it weighed only 500 pounds.

A letter intercepted from the Spanish governor of Puerto Rico in1590 provides evidence that the *Hopewell* carried in its hold as ballast twenty-six pieces of heavy ordnance, which were destined to be transported to the 1587 colony. There is no confirmation of this statement, but David Beers Quinn considers it likely that at least some pieces may have been taken aboard. Nothing is known about the ordnance intended for the 1590 colony, which was supposed to have been carried by the *Moonlight*.

VI. Tools and Equipment

The 1585 Expedition and Related Voyages

Tools, household effects, and similar objects were important items of supply provided any colony. Both Hakluyts made brief suggestions as to what should be included in this category, and Arthur Barlowe supplied the colonists with a cursory knowledge of the tools employed by the Indians. It can be safely assumed, of course, that such things as the knives, hatchets, and axes that Amadas and Barlowe carried with them and which were part of the normal equipment found aboard ship were also provided the colonists. The revictualing and shipbuilding activities carried on by the expedition in the West Indies would have required the use of such basic tools.

The shovels and pickaxes Ralph Lane used in gathering salt at Salinas Bay would also be useful in constructing the fort on Roanoke Island. In planning future endeavors, Lane remarked that he would require his men to carry with them their spades, mattocks, and axes in order to be able to build or dig overnight fortifications for their camps. While sojourning on the island of Puerto Rico, Sir Richard Grenville's men constructed a forge with which they made nails for the pinnace they were building to replace the one that had been lost on the outbound voyage. This forge is described by Hernando Altamirano, the captured Spaniard; it is also mentioned by the Spanish commander at Havana. Such a forge could well have been transported to Roanoke Island, as is suggested by the discovery of a charcoal pit at the site of the 1585 fort, and used to repair tools and weaponry.

A rather complete assortment of carpentry, and possibly masonry, tools must have been brought by the colonists. The houses and the pinnace built by the colonists, as they have been described, would have required such equipment. These tools would likewise have been needed to build the slipway located in a small cove on the east side of Roanoke Island, which, according to Spanish observers, was where the settlers kept their small boats.

There is evidence that the colonists made bricks, although no proof has been found to demonstrate that this material was used in the buildings of either the village or the fort. If bricks were produced, however, then certain masonry tools obviously would have been needed for use in construction. A few miscellaneous items are noted at random in the documents or are illustrated in John White's watercolor drawings and maps. Among these items are sacks in which salt was taken aboard ship at Salinas Bay; barrels used

O   INCHES   4

Brick fragments found at the site of Fort Raleigh on Roanoke Island. Photograph by J. C. Harrington. From J. C. Harrington, "The Manufacture and Use of Bricks at the Raleigh Settlement on Roanoke Island," *North Carolina Historical Review,* XLIV (January, 1967), 8.

to carry fresh water; tents that served as shelters at the temporary encampment in Puerto Rico; "bylboes," or bars, to which leg irons were attached and to which Lane once kept an Indian hostage chained; and handlocks or handcuffs, which were used for the same purpose.

Comfort was certainly not ignored by the leaders of the expedition inasmuch as a number of luxury items were transported aboard ship, some possibly being left with the colonists. Many of these articles seem to have been chosen by Grenville himself or through his instigation. Grenville was described by Enrique Lopez, who had been captured with Pedro Diaz while on board the *Santa Maria de San Vicente,* as a "man of quality" who "is served with much show, and vessels of plate and gold, and servants." Indeed, Hernando Altamirano observed that all the gentlemen of importance had their food served to them on "plate of silver and gold." On one occasion Amadas returned to a native village, just after Grenville and his party had visited it, in order to retrieve a silver cup believed to have been stolen; he burned the village because the Indians did not return the missing cup. Music, furthermore, appears to have been well provided during the voyage. Trumpets, organs, and other instruments were brought aboard ship, and Grenville entertained the Spanish at Isabela, Hispaniola, with a banquet accompanied by trumpet music. Grenville is reported to have greatly enjoyed music while he dined.

In addition to the contemporary documents, there is yet another source of information concerning this phase of the preparations for Lane's colony. In recent years archaeological excavations made at the site of the 1585 fort have unearthed a certain number of artifacts from this period. Chief among these items are a wrought iron sickle comparable to various Elizabethan ex-

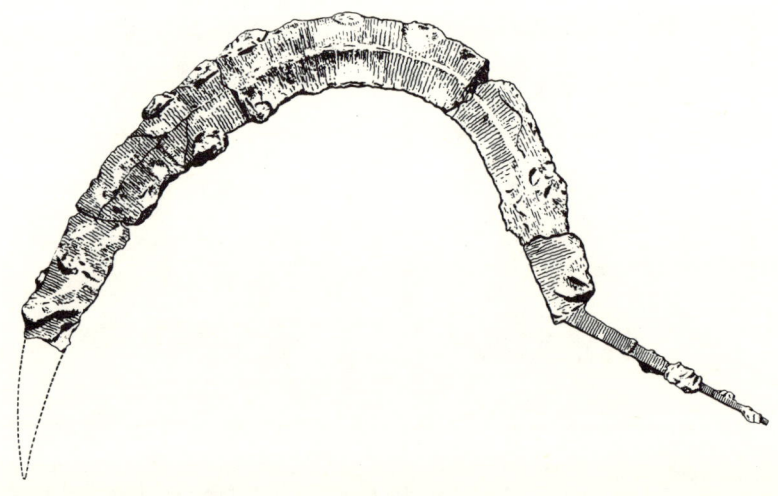

A wrought iron sickle unearthed on Roanoke Island by archaeologists. From Jean Carl Harrington, *Search for the Cittie of Ralegh: Archaeological Excavations at Fort Raleigh National Historic Site, North Carolina* (Washington, D.C.: National Park Service, United States Department of the Interior, 1962), fig. 14.

OBVERSE   REVERSE

OBVERSE   REVERSE

3 CM

Sixteenth-century casting counters found by archaeologists at Fort Raleigh and on the Outer Banks. These privately made "coins" were kept by merchants in a series of boxes or chests to reflect the account balances of their clients as opposed to maintaining written financial records. From Harrington, *Search for the Cittie of Ralegh*, fig. 17.

amples extant in British museums and three sixteenth-century European brass alloy jettons, or casting counters, which were used by the colonists either for calculating sums and quantities or for trade with the Indians. Additional reclaimed articles include fragments of Spanish pottery; a 21½-ounce lump of copper, being either Indian copper ore melted on the spot by Joachim Ganz or European copper brought by the settlers; pieces of Italian enameled pottery; and some handmade iron spikes. In 1709 John Lawson mentioned that he had seen "some old English Coins which have lately been found," as well as the old guns discussed earlier. Talcott Williams, who conducted archaeological investigations on Roanoke Island in the 1890s, spoke of having found several pieces of iron and a corroded nail during his excavations at the site of the fort. J. C. Harrington, formerly an archaeologist with the National Park Service, believes, however, that Williams's pieces of iron were

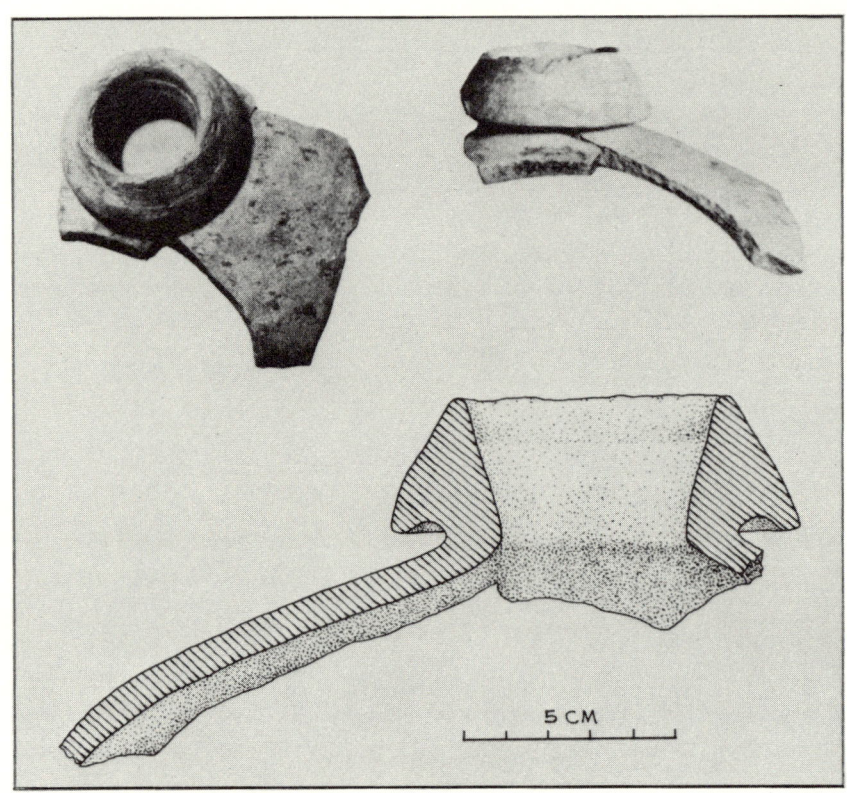

These fragments of a Spanish olive jar (top) and an apothecary jar (bottom), unearthed at Roanoke Island, may have been obtained along with some other supplies in the West Indies by the Roanoke colonists. From Harrington, *Search for the Cittie of Ralegh,* figs. 20, 21.

probably rusty concretions of the subsoil, which are commonly mistaken for iron.

Several fragments of Spanish olive jars have been found that could well be remains from some of the emergency supplies that Sir Francis Drake gave the colony in 1586 or from supplies taken from Spanish prizes captured during the outbound voyage in 1585. Some majolica shards have been identified as having come either from England or the Netherlands; they were likely used for storing medicinal supplies. One interesting fragment of pottery has been associated by one archaeologist with a crucible such as that used by metallurgists of the sixteenth century in making fine gold or silver. The artifact's lack of encrustation indicates that it had never been used. Archaeologist Ivor Noel Hume has suggested that this fragment remains as "a silent yet eloquent commentary on the whole endeavor."

The 1587 Expedition and Related Voyages

There exists very little knowledge concerning the tools and equipment believed to have been taken to Virginia by the 1587 colonists, inasmuch as John White's narrative is the only primary source of information on this subject. The narrative, unlike Ralph Lane's 1585 report, which describes the activities of the colonists, ends with White's return to England. Depositions made by personnel captured aboard prize ships seized by the English are of little value in illuminating the history of the 1587 colony, for the impressed Irishman Darby Glande escaped in the West Indies, and the Spaniard Pedro Diaz was detained in England until 1588, eventually managing to return to Spain. White's 1590 narrative sheds some light on the subject, however, through his comments concerning various articles that still remained at the fort on Roanoke Island. Artifacts, discovered through modern archaeological exploration, yield little positive data on this colony per se, since it has not been determined which group of colonists were associated with any of the specific items.

White's historical narrative of 1590 mentions the finding of discarded "pigs" of lead and "many barres of Iron," the existence of which may be attributed to bullet making and the operation of a forge by the settlers. The forge must have been removed by the colonists, but they would not have been able to handle heavy supplies of iron as well. In 1588 a Spanish expedition discovered barrels half buried in the sand on Roanoke Island; these may have been the remnants of shallow wells lined with wooden barrels for the collection of rainwater. The wells could have been dug anytime between 1585 and 1587. This same Spanish expedition also noted the slipway mentioned earlier.

VII. Books and Instruments

Books and instruments form yet another part of the equipment essential to the colonists in performing the tasks of mapping and investigating the natural and economic resources of their new home. In his *Discourse of Western Planting* Richard Hakluyt, the clergyman, suggested that the Bible, books on religion, and narratives of the discoveries in the West and East Indies be taken as guides. Hernando Altamirano stated that, upon his release from captivity by the English, he was given a Bible, printed in Spanish, which he was enjoined to take to the people of San Juan, Puerto Rico, "in order that the inhabitants there might understand how they had been deceived by their preachers." And the use of an English Bible among the Indians is further described by Thomas Harriot. Historian David Beers Quinn believes that Harriot may have taken a dictionary with him to Virginia in order to match words of the Indian language with their English counterparts. This procedure was, in fact, recommended in a set of instructions prepared for one Thomas Bavin, a surveyor who was to accompany an abortive voyage of 1582 associated with Sir Humphrey Gilbert.

In his *briefe and true report,* Harriot referred to Nicholas Monardes's *Joyfull newes out of the newe founde worlde . . .* (1577), the only volume available in English that described the medicinal plants of North America. It is clear that Harriot had a copy of this work with him for reference. There had also appeared, in 1586, a new edition of *A Niewe Herball,* Henry Lyte's 1578 version of Rembert Dodoen's *Florum . . . Historia* of 1568, which contained the most complete English description of Indian maize, or corn. This work was accessible to Harriot, although it is doubtful that he had a copy with him. It is conceivable, however, that Harriot did have with him numerous works of this type for reference. Ralph Lane reported in his narrative that "Cardes, Bookes and writings" were thrown overboard by Sir Francis Drake's sailors in June, 1586, while they were evacuating the colony.

That Lane and his officers possessed various maps can be inferred from the documents. When Lane wrote Sir Francis Walsingham from Virginia, he mentioned, for example, that the Spanish called Wococon Inlet "St. Mary's," information that he evidently obtained from a Spanish map. The undated sketch map of the Roanoke Island area sent by Lane to Walsingham from Virginia likewise applies the name "saynt maris" to Wococon Inlet. John White's map of eastern North America may have been a compilation of at least four different maps: a Spanish map that included the Bahamas;

Jacques le Moyne's map of Florida, which exhibits remarkable similarities to White's work, done twenty years after le Moyne's departure from the French fort in Florida; John White and Thomas Harriot's map of the present North American coast from the Chesapeake Bay to Cape Lookout, which appears to have been incorporated in miniature; and geographer and mathematician John Dee's map of 1580, which delineates the New World in full. These maps evidently were available for study when White's map was made; there is no indication, however, that White's map was completed prior to his return to England.

Mapping and surveying were two of Harriot's and White's chief functions, and the instruments they used are therefore of considerable interest. Listed in the instructions for Thomas Bavin, the 1582 surveyor—instructions that probably were similar to those followed by Harriot and White in 1585—were the following instruments and materials that would be required:

Three flat watch clocks, of twenty-four- or forty-hour running capacity, with gilded or silvered mechanisms to forestall rust
An instrument to measure the compass variation and another for the declination
A universal dial to determine the sun's true azimuth
A cross-staff (forerunner of the quadrant) to determine the sun's altitude
An "Ephimerides," or almanac, containing the dates of solar and lunar activity and other tables to aid in making navigational calculations
A sailing compass
A "good store of parchments, Paper Ryall, Quills, and Inck, black powder to make ynck, and all sorts of colours to drawe all thinges to life, gumme, pensyll, a stone to grinde colours, mouth glue, black leade, 2 payers of brazen Compasses, And other Instruments to drawe cardes and plottes [maps]"
A plane table for Bavin's surveying instrument

It would seem quite apparent from White's drawings and maps and Harriot's notes (which the latter used to write his *briefe and true report*) that most of the writing materials and related items listed above were among the best available tools with which to perform the professional tasks of the sea, and Harriot himself mentioned the Indians' fascination with the colonists' spring clocks, "perspective glasse," sea compasses, lodestones, "burning glasses," and mathematical instruments. Lane, furthermore, in his letter to Walsingham, spoke of the incident in which the *Tiger* ran aground at Wococon Inlet, causing the loss of provisions, and observed that the vessel lay "beatynge vppon ye shoalle for ye space of ij houres by ye dyalle . . . ," an apparent reference to one of the spring or flat watch clocks described above.

In the sixteenth century a surveyor was capable of mapping entire estates at the rate of 300 to 400 acres per day by employing the then fairly new method of triangulation, which required the use of a theodolite and a plane table. Explorers employed the same method to "describe" the places they visited. One would infer that John White had had some surveying experience,

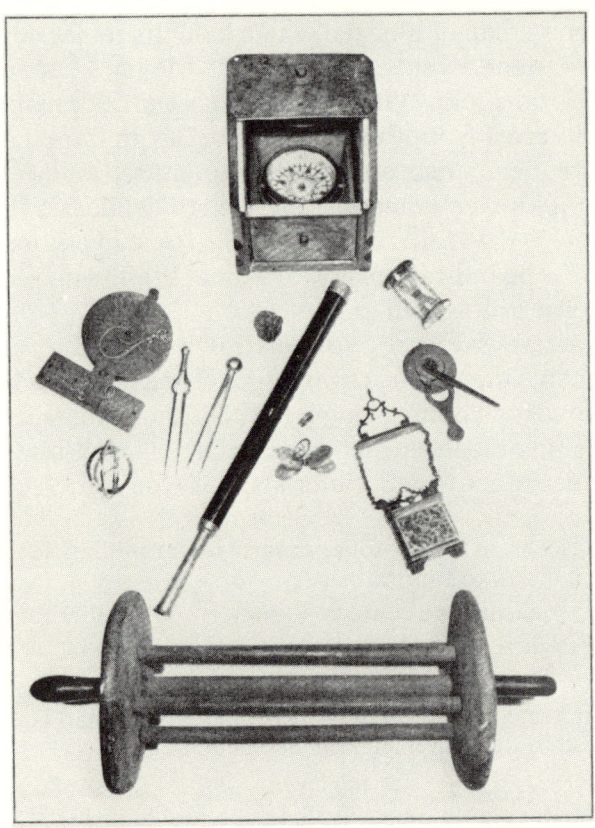

Shown above is a representative collection of instruments of pilotage used by the navigators who took the early colonists to America and the West Indies and who established the trade with India.

Compass
Mounted in gimbals in a square com-
pass-box, fitted in a portable binnacle
with a lantern inside.
(18th century, similar to 16th century)

Lodestone
(17th century)

Half-hour glass
(17th century)

Traverse board
(17th-19th century)

Telescope
(18th century,
similar to 17th
century)

Ring dial
(16th century)

Nocturnal
(17th century)

Two pair of compasses
(17th century)

Pocket dials
(16th century)

Universal ring dial
(17th century)

Lodestone in
brass case
(16th century)

Log-line reel
(17th-19th century)

Examples of the Lead and Line and Dipsie Lead and Line, the fundamental instruments of pilotage for an oceanic navigator approaching land, have been omitted only because of the dictates of space. The Log-chip, Log-line, and Stray-line have been omitted for the same reason. Photograph and information reproduced courtesy trustees of the National Maritime Museum, Greenwich, England.

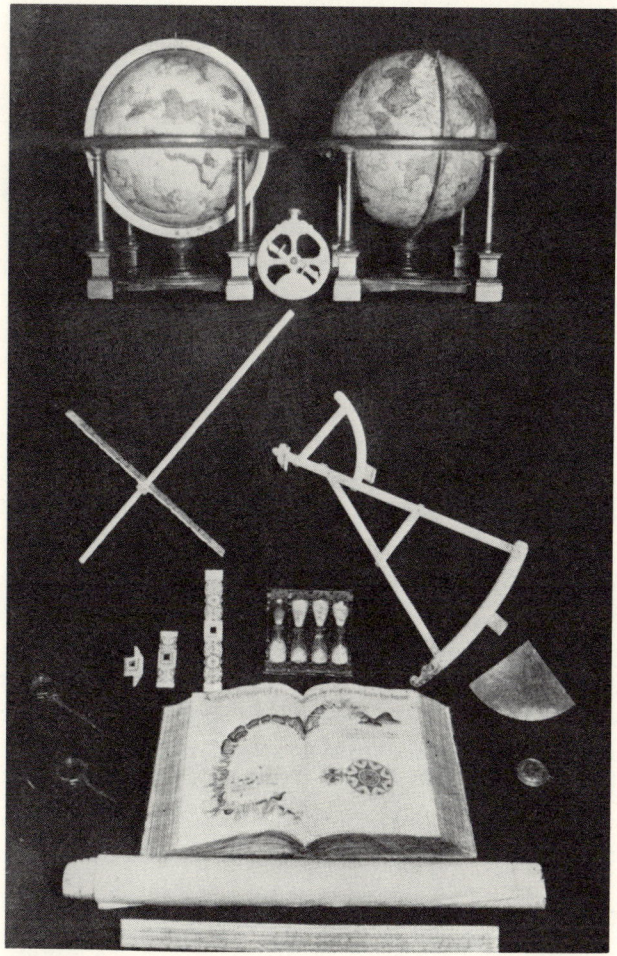

Shown here is another representative collection of navigational instruments used by navigators who took the early colonists to America and the West Indies and established the trade with India.

Celestial globe
(Mercator's, 1551)

Terrestrial globe
(Mercator's, 1541)

Mariner's
astrolabe
(ca. 1585)

Davis quadrant
(17th century)

Cross staff
(17th century;
with 60 cross)

Brass quadrant
(17th century)

5, 15, and 30
crosses

Battery of
half-hour glasses
(17th century)

Dial watch
(16th century)

Two pairs of
circular
compasses
(17th century)

Charts
(17th century)

Gunter's scale
(17th century)

judging from the detail presented in his maps and from his drawings, particularly those of the temporary Puerto Rico encampment and the fortification Lane built while taking salt at Salinas Bay. The mathematics involved in the triangulation method, if beyond White's capabilities, were certainly not beyond those of Thomas Harriot.

The assembling of books and instruments for the 1587 colony may not have been as extensive and thorough as it had been in 1585 under the expert guidance of Thomas Harriot, who, with White, personally conducted studies and mapped the region surrounding the colony. There is no indication in White's 1587 narrative that any preparations approaching those of 1585 were made. In 1590, however, White recorded having found "my bookes torne from the couers, the frames of some of my pictures and Mappes rotten and spoyled with rayne, and my armour almost eaten through with rust." The implication is that White, perhaps with the aid of an unknown assistant, as was specified in the Bavin instructions of 1582, intended to continue the observations and studies begun by Harriot and himself two years earlier. There is a possibility that one of these maps may have been the 1585 map by André Homem, the Portuguese cartographer living in France, which delineates portions of Mexico and the interior of the North American continent. In 1590 White, or Robert Hutton, master of the *Hopewell,* made careful observations of the currents, winds, and other geographic and navigational factors encountered during the voyage. In his narrative of that year White made the earliest recorded observation of the countercurrents, or eddy currents, running against the prevailing flow of the Gulf Stream near the shoreline south of Cape Hatteras. White and Hutton also made numerous soundings in the vicinity of the Carolina Outer Banks.

VIII. The Finances of the Roanoke Voyages

The benefits of Queen Elizabeth's favor gained for Ralegh various offices and lands, producing for him a sizable income and a growing influence at court. As has been previously observed, Ralegh used this wealth and influence to triumph over competitors in obtaining the crown patents of Sir Humphrey Gilbert for the colonization of America.

Substantial financial resources were required to acquire supplies and provisions for a colonizing expedition as well as for a colony, to pay the salaries of personnel, and to rent or acquire adequate shipping. Apart from private enterprise, funds sometimes became available from a direct or indirect state subsidy, from another type of profit-making venture such as privateering, or perhaps by persuading some families of means to undertake to outfit themselves and become colonists.

The Promotional Campaign

In making preparations for the first colony, certain propaganda measures were undertaken. They were designed not only to attract financial support but also to gain the sanction of public opinion. On March 25, 1584, Queen Elizabeth granted to Walter Ralegh letters patent that vested in him the authority to explore, hold, and occupy all lands not possessed by another Christian prince. This grant gave Ralegh the right to receive any royalties that the crown might afterward allow and conferred upon him the responsibilities and duties for the governance and protection of his people.

In the month following his receipt of the grant, Ralegh sent Philip Amadas and Arthur Barlowe on their reconnaissance voyage. The instructions they were to follow in their explorations have not survived, although Barlowe stated in his narrative of the expedition that such a document was personally delivered to them by Ralegh prior to their departure from the river Thames; they subsequently received confirmation of these orders before they departed the West Country. Judging from the course of future events and assuming Amadas and Barlowe conducted themselves according to these instructions, they apparently were directed to search for a desirable location for the planned colony in the latitudes just above the most northern Spanish outposts; to make friendly overtures to the Indians residing in that area; to obtain through trade as many samples of native goods as possible; and, if feasible, to bring back a native of the country to be displayed as a specimen for advertisement, although this last project may well have been instigated by Amadas and Barlowe on a sudden inspiration.

In his report of the voyage, Barlowe gave a pleasing account of the life led by the Indians, their possessions, the friendly relations established with them, and the attractive geographic features of the surrounding territory. This account served as a means of spreading to interested parties favorable information concerning the general location and potential of the colony; and the two Indians brought back, Manteo and Wanchese, appear to have been used for propaganda purposes as well. It is not certain whether the two Indians were taught English or whether Harriot learned their Algonquian dialect, but there is no doubt that some means of communication was developed and that the Indians were able to disseminate stimulating information concerning their homeland. Ralegh's Parliament bill mentions that the Indians had been brought to England and that "singuler great commodities of that Lande" had been shown to members of Parliament.

While Amadas and Barlowe were conducting their explorations, Ralegh commissioned Richard Hakluyt, the clergyman, to write his *Discourse of Western Planting*. This rather substantial pamphlet presented a survey of the reasons why England would profit from the colonization of the New World. It emphasized the role these colonies would play as a source of raw materials for English industries and as a growing market for English goods. It also discussed the possibility of using the settlement as a base of operations for privateering expeditions against the Spanish and as a base for military operations to bring to a halt Spanish expansion on the American continent. Hakluyt also included the usual missionary themes of converting the non-Christian natives and a host of other considerations. The *Discourse* was not published until it was rediscovered in the nineteenth century. That it was written solely for the eyes of the queen, and those with whom she was inclined to share it, appears to be a warranted assumption. Indeed, the title of the work's twentieth chapter states that it is "A Brief Collection of Certain Reasons to Induce Her Majestie and the State to Take A Hand in the Western Voyage and Planting There." The *Discourse* was read by at least some of the expansionists, including Sir Francis Walsingham and the earl of Leicester.

Ralegh was well aware that, in spite of his own substantial private resources, he alone could not hope to bring to a successful conclusion such a colossal undertaking as the colonization of Virginia. To possess the sanction of the queen and to enjoy her financial patronage were two totally different things. The purposes served by the *Discourse* were to persuade Elizabeth to lend her support to the venture by convincing her of the national need for such a project and also to entice her with the expectation of large personal profits. If no significant results along these lines were obtained, at least Hakluyt was rewarded for his efforts by being appointed to the next vacant prebend, or clerical position, at Bristol Cathedral.

The pamphlet entitled "Inducements to the liking of the voyage intended towards Virginia," by the elder Richard Hakluyt, was also written in 1585, probably at Ralegh's request. It presented a conservative estimate of the commercial value of American colonies to English trade. The elder Hakluyt's wide experience with trade and commerce provided Ralegh with a sound practical appraisal of the future potential of colonial trade relationships. It should be noted here that, because of the Spanish threat to English commerce and security in the mid-1580s, the precise location of and details concerning Ralegh's colony were closely guarded secrets; however, no opportunity was lost to proclaim the fact that English settlements were indeed a reality to be reckoned with.

The younger Richard Hakluyt was not idle after presenting his *Discourse* to the queen. Between 1585 and 1590 he obtained from several authors dedications of their works to Ralegh by way of advertisement for the colonizing project. In 1585 Giacopo Castelvetro, publisher for one Guilio Cesare Stella, a citizen of Rome, had printed the latter's work entitled *Columbeidos*, a narrative of the exploits of Christopher Columbus. Castelvetro, who had connections with Sir Francis Walsingham, English secretary of state, and with Lord Burghley, the lord high treasurer, dedicated this edition to Ralegh. The implication was that Castelvetro's English readers should be inspired to undertake similar adventures of their own, as Columbus and Ralegh had done. This approach was perhaps an exaggeration, but Hakluyt, through his friendship with John Wolfe, Castelvetro's printer, visualized this forthcoming book as an opportunity for advertising the Virginia voyages.

In 1587 John Hooker, chief editor of Raphael Holinshed's *Chronicles of England, Scotland and Ireland*, dedicated to Ralegh that portion of the work dealing with "The Irish Historie." Then, in the same year, Martin Basanier published the first edition of the René de Laudonnière narrative, the dedication to which Hakluyt succeeded in obtaining for Ralegh. In 1587 Hakluyt released two works inscribed to Ralegh: a translation from the French of Martin Basanier's edition of Laudonnière's *L'histoire notable de la Floride,* published the previous year; and a new Latin edition of Peter Martyr's *De orbe novo . . . decades octo.* The following year Thomas Harriot, of course, dedicated to Sir Walter his own *briefe and true report of the new found land of Virginia,* and in 1590 Hakluyt obtained an additional inscription to Ralegh in Theodor de Bry's *America.*

It has been suggested that in his zeal to promote Ralegh's Virginia colonizing ventures Richard Hakluyt may have unwittingly contributed to their ultimate failure. Perhaps Hakluyt was too visionary, too preoccupied with the economic and geopolitical potential of prospective English colonies to appreciate the realistic problems that first had to be resolved in order to establish any colony in the American wilderness on a permanent basis. Hakluyt may have unknowingly misled investors and colonists alike as to what they might expect from participating in such a venture, leading them to anticipate quick financial returns on their investments or a vastly different life-style in the colony than they in fact experienced. This could help to explain the adverse sentiments toward Ralegh's expedition apparently voiced by some of the 1585 colonists upon their return to England. Indeed, it appears that apart from John White, only two of the 1585 colonists may have returned with

TO THE RIGHT

WORTHIE AND HONOV-
RABLE, SIR VVALTER RALEGH,

KNIGHT, SENESCHAL OF THE DVCHIES OF

Cornewall and Exeter, and L. Warden of the stannaries in Deuon
and Cornewall. T.B. wisheth true felictie.

AMORE ET VIRTVTE

I R, seeing that the parte of the Worlde, which is betwene the
FLORIDA and the Cap BRETON nowe nammed VIRGI-
NIA, to the honneur of yours most souueraine Layde and Quee-
ne ELIZABETZ, hath ben descouuerd by yours meanes. And
great chardges. And that your Collonye hath been theer established to your great honnor and prayse, and noe lesser proffit vnto the common

a 2

Theodor de Bry's dedication of his 1590 edition of *America* to Sir Walter Ralegh. Reproduced
courtesy British Library Board.

him. On the other hand, Thomas Harriot appears to have realized that the greatest practical value to England of this "new found land" lay in its agricultural potential and natural resources, a fact later borne out by the experience of Jamestown and subsequent colonies along the East Coast. Hakluyt's influence, therefore, may well be an early manifestation of what came to be a typically British characteristic of viewing its colonies abroad strictly in terms of what they could contribute to the economic needs of England and the British Empire as a whole, without consideration of the problems existing overseas from the viewpoint of those who lived there.

After the return of Amadas and Barlowe, the grand family alliance, described earlier, was formed through the marriage of Ralegh's cousin, Barbara Gamage, to Robert Sidney. Sir Walter's next step in his propaganda program was the introduction of a bill in Parliament to confirm the letters patent granted to him by royal prerogative. The associations that resulted from this episode, also previously discussed, were the major benefits derived from this effort. The crown supported Ralegh when he caused the bill to be withdrawn from the agenda because the House of Lords intended to impose certain restrictions on the powers of impressment granted Ralegh in the bill. Neither Ralegh nor Elizabeth desired to initiate any contest of wills between the crown and Parliament over this issue.

General Costs of Putting Ships to Sea

Shipping hired for a voyage in 1585 cost approximately 2 shillings per month per ton, and the average purchase price of a used vessel was about £4 per ton. Judging from Ralegh's sale of the *Ark Royal,* an 800-ton ship sold by him to Queen Elizabeth for £5,000 before it was launched, new shipping would appear to have cost about £6¼ per ton. It is quite unlikely that Ralegh lost any money on this transaction, but it is equally unlikely that he would have realized a profit at the expense of the queen, given their relationship.

Elizabeth made a practice of renting her ships in return for a share in the profits of a venture, but she also accepted the risks involved. Her price for supplying shipping and provisions, up to the value of £500, was one third of the profits. Her partners undertook to pay the wages, post a sizable bond, and, in the case of a trading expedition, ship at least £5,000 worth of goods. During this time, wages for personnel varied from 2 shillings 6 pence per day for a ship captain to 10 shillings a month for a common sailor or soldier, a ship's complement usually averaging one man per 2 tons burden. The capital outlay required to obtain the services of a colonist in 1583 was about £40 per person, this in an economy in which a carpenter's income averaged £15 annually.

The cost of stores with which to furnish a ship approximated a sum equal to the value of the vessel. Expeditions customarily equipped themselves for periods of three months to one year and were expected to provide additional requirements for themselves at their hunting grounds or in the regions in which they traded. Stores were planned to be carried on the basis of pounds sterling per ton and pounds sterling per man, taking into consideration space limitations and basic rations for the crew.

Prize goods seized at sea were ordinarily divided into thirds, one third each for the crew, the victuallers, and the ship owners. If a crew could find no other means of storing or otherwise disposing of its one-third share, it usually sold it to the officers or investors, who often took advantage of such situations. The proceeds were then divided among the men on a proportional basis that enabled each man to receive a share corresponding to his rank. This distribution took place following deck pillage by the crew at the time a prize was seized, and after payment of 5 percent of the spoils to the queen's customs and a 10 percent fee to the lord high admiral.

The Amadas and Barlowe Voyage of 1584

It cannot be determined precisely who, apart from Ralegh, invested in the 1584 voyage of Philip Amadas and Arthur Barlowe. Captain John Smith, whose reliability as a historian is often questioned, stated in his *Historie of Virginia* that Ralegh obtained as assistants Sir Richard Grenville, William Sanderson, and "divers other Gentlemen and Marchants," "who with all speede provided two small Barkes well furnished with all necessaries, under the command of Captaine Philip Amadas and Captaine Barlowe." Simon Fernandes, described by Lane in an August, 1585, letter to Sir Francis Walsingham as "your honours servante," is listed by Barlowe as the "Master of the Admiral," indicating that Walsingham was one of the "divers other Gentlemen and Marchants" mentioned by Smith. In any case, whether Sanderson was involved in 1584 or not, Fernandes is known to have entered Walsingham's service by 1580.

Another possible adventurer in this first expedition was Sir Philip Sidney. In a letter written to Sir Edward Stafford on July 21, 1584, Sidney intimated that Richard Hakluyt had had a certain influence on his association with Sir Humphrey Gilbert. It is possible that Hakluyt helped draw Sidney into the folds of the Ralegh circle, but, of course, Barbara Gamage's recent marriage to Philip Sidney's brother, Robert, likely helped to move things along.

An entry in the Holinshed *Chronicles* referring to the Amadas and Barlowe voyage states that Abraham Fleming, a contributor to the second edition of the *Chronicles,* was supplied his information by someone identified as "G.C." Historian David Beers Quinn suggests that this person could have been either Sir George Carey, who was associated with the later expeditions, or George Carew, Walter Ralegh's cousin and later earl of Totnes. Quinn suspects, however, that "G.C." was most likely William Camden (Guilielmus Camdenus), the historian, with no known personal involvement in the venture. It should also be noted that in Ralegh's letters patent, Elizabeth instructed the lord treasurer, Lord Burghley, to allow Ralegh and his agents to depart from England with any goods they might see fit to take with them for the

William Cecil, the great Lord Burghley, Queen Elizabeth's lord treasurer and close adviser for nearly forty years. Portrait reproduced courtesy National Portrait Gallery, London.

support of the colony, thus implying an indirect subsidy to the expedition in the form of a waiver of any customs duties that might normally have accrued to the crown.

It has been observed that the two ships used in 1584 might possibly have had a total displacement of 250 tons. At the rate of £4 per ton, plus an equal amount usually required to provision such vessels for sea duty, a figure of £2,000 can be estimated as a possible total investment in the Amadas and Barlowe expedition (see Table 3, p. 93). The only revenue that might have been derived from the venture would have been in the nature of goods bartered from the Indians for sale in England; but, because of the exploratory nature of the voyage, it is doubtful that such trading was done on a scale larger than that necessary to acquire a sampling of the native products of the area. In his narrative, Barlowe made no mention of any attempt by either ship to conduct privateering activities during the course of the voyage. However, one Richard Butler declared long afterward that Amadas set sail for the Azores in the hope of taking a prize, although he returned home six weeks later empty handed.

The Grenville Expedition and Lane Colony of 1585

The 1585 expedition appears to have been financed from four separate sources: the queen, Ralegh's associates and coadventurers, Ralegh himself, and revenues obtained from privateering conducted both before and during the expedition. Elizabeth's marked generosity toward Ralegh, which generally took the form of appointments to offices with lucrative incomes, has already been discussed. With respect to investments specifically involving the 1585 expedition, however, certain additional insights can be gleaned. A royal signet letter, dated February 2, 1585, addressed to Ambrose Dudley, earl of Warwick and master of ordnance at the Tower of London, instructs him to release to Ralegh or Ralegh's agents four lasts of powder in double-charged casks, valued at £400. This was, indeed, a direct subsidy paid from the crown. As has been previously observed, it might well be in conjunction with the delivery of this powder that the Thames incident, involving Amadas and the Thames watermen, occurred, especially since John Powell, Warwick's surveyor of ordnance, was in the boat with Amadas at the time.

Six days after this order for powder was signed, Elizabeth wrote to Sir John Perrot, lord deputy of Ireland, instructing him to relieve Ralph Lane of his duties, with pay, for more pressing service at the queen's discretion. Lane's duties during his absence were to be performed by his lieutenant, who was to be paid by the crown and assisted by twenty horsemen and forty footmen. An endorsement on the letter stated that Lane's appointment was "Graciously giuen him by her Majestie in consideration of his redye vndertakinge ye Voyage to Virginia for Sir Walter Raughley, at her Majesties commaundement." Ralegh was thereby provided a second direct subsidy from the queen, regardless of who instigated the request for Lane's services. Serving as lieutenant of the expedition, Lane likely would have received the usual wage of that rank, about £3 per month; but there were, of course, no precedents for the salary of a governor of a colony. At £3 per month for the sixteen months between April, 1585, and July, 1586, his salary would have added another £48 to Elizabeth's investment.

As still further evidence of the crown's support for the Virginia ventures, Elizabeth gave Ralegh the use of the *Tiger,* a 150-ton Royal Navy vessel, worth an additional £600 at the £4-per-ton rate. This, taken with the gunpowder and Lane's salary, would place the queen's total investment in the Grenville-Lane expedition at about £1,050, at a time when her total annual revenue was about £350,000 per year.

Ralegh's associates and coadventurers not only helped finance the 1585 voyage, but some of them even became members of the expedition and colonists. Sir Richard Grenville's principal contribution to the venture appears to have been in organizing the shipping, obtaining provisions, and engaging the personnel, chiefly in the Bideford area. Grenville assumed these tasks late in December, 1584. His brother-in-law, John Stukeley, who accompanied him on the expedition, may have contributed toward the provisioning of the *Tiger.* There is no evidence, however, that Grenville personally invested any money or materials in the expedition, although he did earn profits from the privateering activities in which he engaged during the voyage.

There is also an indication that Grenville had some contacts with London merchants through one Master Middleton, probably Thomas Middleton, a London grocer, who brought his son to Grenville at Plymouth shortly before the expedition sailed. Thomas Middleton was definitely involved in the later series of Virginia voyages and was associated with a number of enterprising London merchants, including John Watts, Henry Cletherow, Robert Cobb,

Thomas Cordell, John Stokes, and Paul Bayning. Some of these men, such as Cletherow, who was an ironmonger and rope merchant, had special interests in shipping and could invest crucial materials required for outfitting ships.

Another link between the 1585 expedition and the London merchants is found in the person of Thomas Harvey, the London grocer. As is apparent from depositions made in a 1591 court case involving Harvey and his wife, Harvey evidently was not a very efficient businessman. Listed by Lane as one of the 1585 colonists, he served as the chief merchant for the colony. He claimed to have spent the greater part of his own fortune on more than just one of the ventures and even to have borrowed additional resources to support them. Quinn believes that if Harvey did perform such transactions, it was most likely done in the form of private investments in goods he planned to barter and trade for his own benefit, an activity not uncommon for a chief merchant of that period. It is possible that Harvey was referring to expenses incurred in outfitting himself for the voyage or, less likely, in adventuring money or goods to the expedition itself. Harvey implied in this deposition that he did not receive a satisfactory settlement of his accounts with Ralegh or the other adventurers. In helping with the preparations for the voyage, which his role as chief merchant would have required him to do, Harvey must have worked closely with Martin White, Ralegh's factor at Plymouth and one of his principal agents in the South West.

The intimate relationship of William Sanderson with Ralegh has been noted. There is, however, no direct mention of Sanderson's association with the 1585 venture. Certain biographical data, possibly written by his son after Sanderson's death in 1631, suggest that Sanderson may have acted as a financial manager for Ralegh, becoming in time his most important link with the London merchants. This brief source states that Sanderson, after marrying Ralegh's niece, "did manage his [Ralegh's] affaires all the tyme of his prosperity," often borrowing funds for him. It has already been mentioned that Sanderson was considered by John Smith, a rather dubious authority, to have contributed to the 1584 voyage. Apart from this reference, nothing factual is known about Sanderson's involvement in 1585, although there is room for a great deal of speculation.

In 1584 Sir Francis Walsingham was a supporter of the London Merchant Adventurers, which possibly provides yet another connection between that group and the 1585 Roanoke voyage. At least three men in Walsingham's service went on that voyage, but none of them remained with the colony. Their names were Simon Fernandes, the chief pilot; one called Atkinson; and another named Russel. There is additional evidence that Martin Laurentson, a Dane assigned by Frederick II of Denmark to the service of Queen Elizabeth to learn the art of naval warfare, went on this expedition under Grenville at the instigation of Walsingham. From Virginia, Ralph Lane wrote Walsingham at least three letters in which he discussed freely the problems encountered in the voyage, made complaints against various members of the expedition—especially Grenville and Thomas Cavendish—and expressed himself in the manner of an employee reporting to his employer on the progress of his assignment. He even asked the secretary to read a lengthy report that he had sent to Ralegh, a document that unfortunately has not survived. And in one of these letters he apparently forwarded to Walsingham a small sketch map of the Roanoke Island area.

Upon his return to Plymouth, Grenville wrote Walsingham to acquaint him with the success of the voyage. In the letter, Grenville actually named Walsingham as an adventurer in the expedition, stating that he was "gladde that my happe is to yealde your honor the retorne of your adventure with some gagne." He added that he was "persuaded that god hathe bene the rather favorable vnto me for that your honour hathe bene an adventurer therein" and promised to report more fully in person after his arrival at court. Walsingham's biographer, Conyers Read, minimized the significance of these statements by Grenville, regarding them merely as terms of respect to the secretary made in deference to his proximity to the queen's ear. In light of the evidence now available, however, Quinn shares the opposite point of view, declaring that when Lane addressed Walsingham in a letter as "your honor and ye reste of ye mooste honorable adventurerres," there could be little doubt as to his intended meaning.

Other than the previously mentioned relationship between Sir Philip Sidney and the adventurers, there is no additional evidence that Sidney contributed to the 1585 expedition. Lane wrote him from Virginia, although this correspondence appears to have been prompted more by friendship than by any other motive. Sir George Carey, however, was very likely a contributor to the venture. As vice admiral of Hampshire and governor of the Isle of Wight, he was involved in the disposition of certain goods taken from a prize captured by one of Ralegh's ships, probably the *Roebuck,* prior to the departure of Grenville's fleet. Carey was definitely connected with later Roanoke voyages, but this association may have begun with his membership on the committee in Parliament that was to consider Ralegh's bill.

Thomas Cavendish, who served as high marshal of the expedition, was certainly an investor. Lane recalled in his reminiscences of the voyage that Cavendish "Furnished out a ship wherein he went as Captaine with Sir Richard Grenville to Virginia." This statement suggests that this vessel, the *Elizabeth,* was Cavendish's own ship, which would have doubled his investment. A 50-ton pinnace, according to 1588 prices, might have been worth £200, depending on its age and equipment. Since the cost of victualing a ship normally approximated the value of the vessel, Cavendish's investment may have reached £400. His connection with the "Cavendish notes" involved him even further in the preparations for the expedition, and the contents of the notes had a direct bearing on his duties as high marshal.

Both Ralegh's brother, Carew Ralegh, and his half brother, Adrian Gilbert, may have contributed to the financing of the 1585 expedition. There is reason to believe that they shared in the value of the ivory tusks that came from the prize Grenville captured during his return trip to England. Bernard Drake also obtained ivory during the 1585 voyage. It may be safely assumed from this evidence that the two men were indeed associated in the financing of the 1585 voyages. Robert Sidney, Anthony Rowse, and others listed in connection with Ralegh's bill in Parliament are all regarded as likely to have had a vested interest in the venture.

Two other men might possibly have been investors in Sir Walter Ralegh's 1585 colony. One is Peregrine Bertie, Lord Willoughby de Eresby, a diplomatic envoy to Denmark, who appears to have had a personal interest in the results of Lane's colony. The second is Lord Charles Howard, baron of Effingham, who also happened to be lord high admiral of England. In his narrative, Lane referred to Croatoan as "my lord Admirals Island." Ralegh corroborated Howard's role in a statement to Sir Robert Cecil in 1602. Ralegh said that Howard had "freedome and an interest in the countrye," which would indicate that Howard had more at stake than merely the official fees he collected. As lord high admiral, he may have received, in addition to his own personal investment, fees totaling as much as £5,000 for his one-tenth levy on the total income derived from the 1585 privateering activities.

Charles Howard of Effingham, lord high admiral of England and an investor in the 1585 expedition. Engraving from Edmund Lodge, *Portraits of Illustrious Personages of Great Britain* (London: William Smith, 12 volumes in 8, 1835), IV.

Little can be deduced concerning Sir Walter Ralegh's personal investment in the 1585 venture or, for that matter, in any of the expeditions. In February, 1585, Bernardino de Mendoza, former Spanish ambassador to England, wrote King Philip II of Spain from France that Ralegh had purchased two 120-ton Dutch flyboats and two 40-ton barks and was having built for himself four new pinnaces of 20 to 30 tons. At the £4-per-ton cost of used shipping, the flyboat and barks would have cost Ralegh about £1,280. At the going price of £6¼ per ton for new shipping, his expenditures for building the four new pinnaces would have ranged between £500 and £750. The value of the pinnace lost by the *Tiger* on the way to Virginia has been estimated by one authority at £200. Of these vessels, it is possible that the two 120-ton ships, one of the 40-ton barks, and two of the new pinnaces were used in the 1585 expedition—a possible total of from £1,370 to £1,495 worth of shipping provided at Ralegh's expense. At least the *Roebuck* and the *Dorothy* of the Grenville fleet are known to have been Ralegh's ships. The two pinnaces were probably his as well. Apart from these facts, no other specific information is known concerning Sir Walter's own personal financial investment.

Adventurers who supported the 1585 expedition expected to receive a return on their investments from privateering, and it is certain that such a prospect was indeed Ralegh's intention. This method of obtaining a return on investments, together with the hope of finding riches in Virginia, were Ralegh's only practical means of encouraging the participation of private capital. To these subscribers, the act of planting a colony was as secondary as it was to John Watts in 1590 when White revisited the Roanoke settlement site. It was difficult for such businessmen to see how dividends from a colonial project could be anticipated in advance in the absence of the discovery of rich minerals that they could exploit. Such a discovery was very uncertain, however, and privateering remained the principal attraction. A long-term outlay of capital was required in the meantime, and the great risks involved meant that any failures demanded a repetition of that outlay. Additionally, the necessary annual dispatch of provisions represented a continual drain upon investors' resources, for supply squadrons were a crucial necessity until a colony could be made self-supporting. Indeed, the means by which such a colony could be made self-sustaining in the shortest length of time was through the discovery of some rich mineral or precious metal or, as was eventually learned at Jamestown, by planting a money crop suitable to the region and capable of being profitably exported.

A summary of the privateering activities engaged in prior to and during the 1585 expedition will reveal the extent of the income received from this venture by the investors. There is evidence that at least one of Ralegh's ships was privateering in the English Channel before the departure of Grenville's fleet. The *Waterhound* of Briell was captured, possibly by the *Roebuck,* and both the master and the pilot of the vessel were impressed into Ralegh's service and forced to make the voyage to Virginia with Grenville. The *Waterhound* was laden with wine, which, together with the ship, appears to have been worth approximately £1,000. A ship belonging to Ralegh, with John Clarke serving as captain, also took as a prize a French vessel carrying a cargo of linen and wheat, and the *Roebuck* was again most likely the privateer inasmuch as John Clarke served as its captain during the 1585 voyage to Virginia. As to the *Waterhound* the records imply that Ralegh struck a bargain in the courts and, because of his influence, was allowed to keep it. It appears, on the other hand, that he was forced to return the French prize, although he may have profited in some manner from its contents before restoring the ship to its owners.

The capture of a prize by the 1585 expedition is first mentioned in a report to Philip II from Bernardino de Mendoza, who identified the ill-fated ship as a Spanish Newfoundlander, possibly a fishing vessel. Mendoza stated that the crew was killed and the vessel sent to Ireland. His report is without any corroboration, however, and may well be unfounded. Definitive prize taking began in the West Indies immediately after the new pinnace had been launched at Puerto Rico. On the night of May 23, 1585, an empty Spanish frigate was captured in the Mona Channel, and another was seized the following morning. The latter prize was laden with "good and rich fraight," including Spanish hostages who were ransomed for "good round summes."

The Spanish confirmed these captures in at least two sources, adding that the latter ship had a heavy cargo of cloth and other merchandise belonging to one Lorenzo de Vallejo and had strayed from the Spanish Santo Domingo fleet. There is a remote possibility that it may have been a French vessel employed to supply a group of French merchants on the coast of Hispaniola, with whom Fernandes's friend Alanson may have been associated. Hernando de Altamirano was one of the hostages whom Grenville impressed from this second frigate. Altamirano later reported in his deposition that at San German, Puerto Rico, Grenville attempted unsuccessfully to obtain livestock in exchange for the hostages. Quinn interprets this as an attempt to help provide cover for the local inhabitants, who did trade with the English. It has already been observed that sugar, hides, ginger, pearls, and tobacco were procured at Puerto Rico, probably for sale in England.

The one great prize of the venture was taken during the return voyage from Virginia to England. It was the *Santa Maria de San Vicente,* flagship of the Spanish Santa Domingo squadron, which had been separated from the rest of the fleet by a storm. On board the ship were two men who later made depositions that shed considerable light upon the affair: Enrique Lopez, who described the encounter and evaluated the cargo captured, and Pedro Diaz, the pilot of the *Santa Maria,* whom Grenville retained as pilot for the 1586 voyage to Virginia. Lopez's account is the more valuable inasmuch as he gave details of the capture. Lopez reported that Grenville boarded the vessel and confiscated about 40,000 ducats worth of gold, silver, and pearls, plus the personal valuables of the passengers. Included in this seizure was the *Santa Maria's* cargo, which consisted of 8,000 arrobas (202,880 pounds) of sugar, 7,000 hides, 100,500 pounds of ginger, and other merchandise valued at 80,000 ducats. Lopez estimated the total value of the prize to be 120,000 ducats, not counting the 300- to 400-ton ship itself, which could add another £1,400. Mendoza stated that cochineal and ivory also comprised part of the confiscated goods.

Grenville denied, however, that there was any gold, silver, or pearls aboard the *Santa Maria,* except for the small amount that "belonged to private persons who were passengers into Spain from St. Domingo." He estimated the total value of the ship's cargo to be 40,000 to 50,000 ducats. The ducat was worth about six English shillings in 1583 or 1584. This figure would place Lopez's total estimate at £36,000 and Grenville's at £12,000 to £15,000. Quinn suggests that if the unregistered cargo and luggage were counted, the Spanish estimates might reach 160,000 ducats, or £48,000.

An English document casts some doubt upon the reliability of Grenville's own claims. On December 9, 1585, Sir Walter Ralegh's half brother, Adrian Gilbert, wrote to Dr. Julius Caesar, judge of the High Court of Admiralty, affirming "vpon my credyt" that "olofantes tethe" came with Sir Richard Grenville and that "besydes those that I have there were .4.[4] more one Sir Walter Raleigh had, & one Carrew Raleighe & the other .2.[2] Sir Richard Grenville had." Gilbert added that this statement could be confirmed by "a dozen honest persons that knew the same," including Sir Walter himself. In a letter to the queen, possibly from William Herlle, one of her diplomatic agents, is a report that letters from Spain estimated the value of this prize at 600,000 ducats, or £180,000. Herlle's report probably exaggerated the valuation, although it does imply that the queen was accustomed to receiving more than her share in the returns on an investment and even hints that much of the cargo was brought into England unregistered. For example, Sir Lewis Stukeley, son of Grenville's brother-in-law, John Stukeley, who accompanied Grenville on the 1585 voyage, charged in an allegation on behalf of his father's estate that Ralegh had cheated Grenville and him and had confessed to the value of the *Santa Maria*'s cargo as being £50,000. Still another contemporary estimate of the value of the prize, found in an Austrian manuscript collection, declared it to be worth 1 million ducats, or £300,000.

Of all these conjectures of the worth of the *Santa Maria*, it is likely that Enrique Lopez's estimate of £36,000, plus an additional £12,000 for unregistered cargo and £1,400 for the ship itself, is the most reliable. Grenville was undoubtedly attempting to minimize the value of the returns, possibly already having surreptitiously unloaded the bullion on another part of the English coast in order to smuggle it into London. Elizabeth apparently confiscated all the pearls that were captured. If Lopez's figure is accepted, it is possible that the total revenue derived from the 1585 expedition reached £51,000, representing the sum total of all revenues seized from the *Santa Maria* and the prizes taken in the West Indies and the English Channel but not including any goods that might have been traded in the West Indies or any produce and goods that might have been brought back from Virginia. The following table summarizes the various estimates for privateering income from the 1585 Grenville expedition and indicates the valuations believed most likely to be accurate.

Table 1
ESTIMATES OF THE VALUE OF PRIVATEERING INCOME FROM THE 1585 GRENVILLE EXPEDITION

	Ducats	Pounds Sterling
1. *Waterhound* of Briell—taken by the *Roebuck*	3,333	1,000
2. Spanish Newfoundlander (fishing boat) Report discounted	-0-	-0-
3. First Spanish frigate—empty (est. 80 tons)		300
4. Second Spanish frigate—est. 80 tons		300
Estimate of cloth and other merchandise		400
5. *Santa Maria de San Vicente:*		
a. Lopez estimate—cargo value	120,000	36,000
—unregistered cargo (Quinn)	40,000	12,000
—value of ship, est. at 350 tons	4,667	1,400
		51,400

According to customary division of prizes in the late sixteenth century, the following distribution would have occurred:

Her Majesty's customs (5 percent)	£ 2,570
Lord high admiral's fee (10 percent)	5,140
Crew's share (one third of remainder)	14,563
Owners and victuallers (two thirds of remainder)	29,127
	£51,400

The £29,127 received by the owners and victuallers is likely the sum total of profit from this 1585 expedition.

It is unlikely that Sir Walter Ralegh rented any of the ships employed in his expedition. He probably either owned them himself or used the ships adventured by other individuals in return for a share of the profits. The following table provides the best estimates of tonnage and values for the seven ships known to have participated.

Table 2
SHIPS OF THE 1585 GRENVILLE EXPEDITION

			Lower Estimate		Upper Estimate	
Name	Owner	Cost In Pounds Sterling Per Ton	Tons	Value In Pounds Sterling	Tons	Value In Pounds Sterling
Tiger	Elizabeth I	4	150	600	150	600
Roebuck	Ralegh	4	140	560	140	560
Lion	Raymond (part owner)	4	120	480	120	480
Dorothy	Ralegh	4	40	160	50	200
Elizabeth	Cavendish	4	40	160	50	200
pinnace	Ralegh	6¼	20	125	30	187½
pinnace	Ralegh	6¼	20	125	30	187½
			530	2,210	570	2,415

Used shipping: 490 to 530 tons, worth £1,960 to £2,040
New shipping: 40 to 60 tons, worth £250 to £375

Using the upper limits set forth above, which would increase expenses and minimize profits on any final balance sheet, the total value of the new and used shipping would have been about £2,415. Quinn conservatively estimates this expense at £2,000. The total cost of supplying and victualing a ship for a six-month voyage has been estimated as being the same value as that of the ship. This would add another £2,415 to the 1585 expense account.

On the basis of the required quantity of daily rations of food and drink (discussed in chapter 4) and prices known to have paid for such items during the period, it has been estimated that the cost of victualing crewmen was 7 pence per man per day. Quinn considers the complement of Grenville's force, including the 108 colonists, to have been about 600 men. According to the records, the expedition was away from England for 191 days, of which the 108 colonists were present for the first 137 days. At the rate of 7 pence per man per day, the minimum quantity of rations likely to have been consumed by the colonists during the voyage would have cost about £431 (137 days for 108 men @ 7 pence per day = £431 11 shillings). These provisions would have been over and above the quantity of stores and equipment carried for the sustenance of the colony after the departure of the fleet for England. Included in this calculation, furthermore, is the assumption that all the colonists consumed the same fare that a common seaman was allotted. The "gentlemen of quality" and higher-ranking officers would, of course, have provided themselves with whatever they wished in the way of comforts and luxuries, depending upon the space available aboard ship.

It would be interesting to determine the cost of the various types of equipment furnished Ralph Lane and his men, but such a determination can only be approximated because, as has been seen, the colonists made only isolated references in the documents to their tools, weapons, books, instruments, and other equipment. William Robert Scott, an authority on the activities of the various trade and plantation companies of the fifteenth and sixteenth centuries, has calculated that in 1583 it required approximately £40 to equip and outfit a colonist. Using Scott's formula, Lane's 108 men would have cost Ralegh and his associates about £4,320. It is assumed that whatever would be required by the colonists over and above those supplies furnished by the £40 sum, they would be expected to provide for themselves at the site of the colony. Of course, additional supplies and equipment would have to follow periodically until the colony became economically stable.

Based on these estimates, it would appear, therefore, that the Grenville expedition and Lane colony of 1585 cost about £9,581. A different method of calculating shipping costs, interestingly, yields similar results. Michael Oppenheim, an authority on the costs of ships and men in the Elizabethan period, has estimated that it cost an average of £1$\frac{16}{100}$ per ton burden per month to keep a ship at sea in the late sixteenth century. If this figure is applied to the 570 tons of shipping used in 1585 during a six-and-one-half-month period at sea, a figure of £4,298 results. Adding to this the £4,320 cost of equipping the colonists and the £432 cost of providing them with rations during the outbound voyage, a total estimate of £9,049 is obtained. In view of the nature of this colonizing venture, the usual or customary level of expenses is likely to have proved inadequate, and it would not be surprising to learn that the cost of the Grenville expedition and Lane colony exceeded £10,000.

The Bernard Drake Expedition of 1585

Bernard Drake's 1585 expedition to Newfoundland was originally planned as a follow-up supply squadron for the Lane colony, but at the last moment Queen Elizabeth directed it to Newfoundland for the purpose of delivering to English fishermen there royal orders prohibiting them from selling their catches to the Spanish. Elizabeth also granted the expedition permission to engage in privateering during the voyage. The adventurers known to have invested in this voyage, apart from Sir Walter Ralegh, were the queen, Bernard Drake, Amyas Preston, and John Marshall of London and the Middle Temple.

The *Golden Royal,* which served as the admiral of Bernard Drake's expedition to Newfoundland, was a 110-ton ship with an approximate value of £440. Preston, the vessel's principal victualler, invested between £100 and £200 in its preparation, according to several of the depositions submitted in a court case he instigated to recoup his share of the profits derived from the prizes. Preston ultimately claimed only a 10 percent share in the revenue of the expedition, which he valued at £20,000. This ratio means that the total investment in the *Golden Royal* was between £1,000 and £3,000. The lower figure of £1,000 is a more reasonable estimate of the sum required for putting a 110-ton ship to sea, assuming that the cost of victualing and equipping a ship was equal to the value of the vessel. If Preston were correct, however, in claiming that his £300 equaled 10 percent of the total investment, then the £3,000 figure would indicate the involvement of more than one ship in the venture. There is evidence that Ralegh's ship *Job* might have been with this expedition in the North Atlantic. It is known to have put into Breton port with a 16-ton load of cedar wood, which had probably been transshipped from the *Lion* of Grenville's fleet.

As to the other adventurers, the queen gave her £120 investment to Ralegh as a consolation prize for having diverted his expedition from Virginia, thereby assigning to him all profits she might otherwise have received. John Marshall merely stated that he was part victualler in the *Golden Royal.* Bernard Drake's percentage in the investment is unknown, as is Ralegh's. What is indicated by these depositions is that Drake and Ralegh seized the largest share of the profits and that Preston was obliged to go to a court of law in order to obtain his 10 percent.

Bernard Drake met George Raymond aboard the *Lion* somewhere in Newfoundland waters as the latter was returning to England from Virginia. The

Shown in this painting by Darrell McClure is a typical rendezvous of ships at sea. Such a rendezvous was effected by Bernard Drake and George Raymond off Newfoundland in 1585.

two men apparently entered into a consortship for conducting privateering activities. Various depositions filed in connection with a resulting law case generally agree that the prizes taken numbered about sixteen or seventeen Portuguese fishing vessels and four or five other ships from Brazil and India laden with sugar, wine, ivory, and some gold. The depositions vary widely, however, in regard to the total value of the prizes, with estimates ranging from a conservative £10,000 to a probably exaggerated £60,000. One of the depositions listed two of the sugar-laden vessels as being worth £9,000 and £10,000 respectively, whereas John Drake, son of Bernard Drake, believed four of the ships to have a value not exceeding £8,000.

The litigation concluded with Raymond being awarded 60,000 fish, 16 tons of oil, and 1,000 chests of sugar as a lawful prize by the High Court of Admiralty. Bernard Drake was granted 100 chests of sugar valued at £380, which would make Raymond's sugar worth £3,800. A record indicates that 1,000 fish were sold for £5 in 1588, at which rate Raymond's fish would have been worth £300. In 1587 oil sold for £20 per ton, which would have given Raymond's 16 tons of the commodity a value of £320. The total value of his interest in the venture thus approximated £4,420. Under these conditions, it is probably safe to assume that Preston's estimate of £20,000 was a reasonable, and perhaps even low, valuation of the prizes. Of this sum, £3,000 would have been paid for the queen's customs and the lord admiral's one-tenth share, leaving £17,000 to be divided in the customary manner. After the crew received its one-third share, or £5,666, the two-thirds share claimed by the adventurers would have been £11,332, which, after deducting their expenses of £3,000, would have netted them about £8,332, or nearly a 300 percent profit.

In the dedication of his edition of René de Laudonnière's *L'histoire notable de la Floride*, Martin Basanier declared that Ralegh spent 60,000 crowns on the 1584 and 1585 expeditions. Quinn gives a contemporary valuation of this figure as £20,000, suggesting that it represents not only Ralegh's expenditures but also the total investment of all the adventurers in the two voyages. He adds that this was a high, yet possible, sum.

Ralegh's Supply Ship of 1586

Ralegh's supply ship of 1586 was a vessel of 100 tons and was likely worth about £400 at £4 per ton. According to the usual scale, as previously mentioned, it probably cost Ralegh some £800 or a little more to put to sea, which he did "at his own charge." It was a supply ship "fraighted with all maner of things in most plentiful maner for the supplie and relief of his Colonie then remaining in Virginia" and as such was evidently loaded with provisions and equipment that required a considerable outlay of capital. It may have been carrying some of the ordnance and other supplies for which John Arundell was sent to England from Roanoke Island to obtain. Whatever these supplies included, however, Ralegh recovered most of it inasmuch as the ship returned home without finding the colony. Ralph Lane and his men had already returned to England with Sir Francis Drake. An estimated £800 is a reasonable figure for the total expense of the supply ship's voyage.

The Grenville Expedition of 1586

Grenville prepared his 1586 expedition primarily at Bideford, although circumstantial evidence suggests that most of the shipping departed from Plymouth. From reliable estimates that six or seven ships, varying from 60 to 150 tons each, comprised the expedition, it would appear that four or five of the smaller vessels were probably prepared in Plymouth and sailed from that port. The exact combined tonnage of the six or seven vessels is not known, although a reasonable expectation based on the 1585 experience might suggest one ship at 150 tons, one at 120 tons, one at 100 tons, and three at 60 tons, for a total 550 tons. This tonnage would represent a value of £2,200 at £4 per ton. At the same standard rate of valuation, these vessels would have cost an additional £2,200 to equip and supply, not counting the cost of supplies for the colony in Virginia. Assuming that Grenville left fifteen men in Virginia as a holding party, the cost of equipment and provisions necessary to supply them adequately at £40 per person would have totaled £600. The balance of the supplies would have been returned to England, leaving a probable total cost of the expedition and colonists at about £5,000.

Among the adventurers associated with this expedition, apart from Ralegh and Grenville, whose shares in the venture are unknown, Ralegh's half brother, Sir John Gilbert, appears to have been definitely interested. Martin White, Ralegh's factor at Plymouth, and Sir John Gilbert seized 20 tons of wine from the French ship *Susanne* while it was anchored in the port of Southampton. They stated that the wine was for the "provisioning of the ships" of Sir Walter Ralegh. Carew Ralegh, Sir Walter's brother, also appears to have taken part in the venture by attempting to raise money from the Merchant Adventurers in Exeter. The Exeter group declined to participate, however, since it was involved at that time with one of John Davis's voyages in search of the Northwest Passage. The incident does leave room for speculation that other organizations in Devonshire, such as the one in Barnstaple, were approached. John Norris of Barnstaple was a subscriber to the venture and in October, 1585, was issued letters of reprisal for five ships, some of which may have sailed with Grenville. Depositions from the admiralty court proceedings involving the distribution of the goods taken from the prizes seized during the voyage suggest that one Richard Willett of Bideford may also have had an investment in the expedition.

Six prizes were captured off Cape Finistere: the *Angel* of Topsham, from which was taken a quantity of wine and oil belonging to Breton merchants; the *Peter,* or *Brave,* a Norman ship; the *Martin Johnson,* a Dutch flyboat taken by Captain Arthur Facy; the *Julian* of St. Brieuc, a 60-ton vessel with a full hold of mixed cargo; a Spanish bark laden with hides, taken near Villa Franca; and another Spanish frigate, captured with the aid of some unknown English privateer.

Willett stated in a deposition that the 60 tons of cargo aboard the *Julian* were divided as follows:

Lord high admiral	6 tons
John Norris of Barnstaple	11 tons
Ralegh and Grenville	35 tons
Richard Willett	8 tons

Quinn estimates the cargo of the *Julian* to have had a value of £220, a figure he calculated from Willett's statement that his share was worth £31 9s. Quinn suggests, however, that the figures are not above suspicion, since no portion was reserved for the crew. It is also apparent that no customs dues were paid. The Breton merchants, whose goods these were, claimed their value to have been £294 2s, perhaps a more reliable figure. In December, 1586, the High Court of Admiralty ordered Richard Willett to return to these merchants some of the wine and oil he had taken from the *Angel* of Topsham, the percentage of the total cargo he was allowed to retain not being indicated. In June, 1587, the admiralty court ordered Grenville to make restitution of the goods he had taken from the *Martin Johnson,* although Grenville appears to have delayed for a considerable time before complying with the order.

From these court documents, no accurate conclusion can be drawn concerning the total value of the prizes taken during the Grenville voyage of

1586. The value of each prize was not recorded in the documents. Quinn contends, however, that "With three Dutch and two Spanish prizes Grenville is likely to have paid both his own way and that of the supply ship, even though he had to restore some of his gains to the French and Dutch."

Assuming that Grenville's expedition of 1586 obtained sufficient revenue from the captured prizes to offset the amounts invested, as proposed above, it would have cleared £5,000 after paying the lord high admiral's 10 percent, the queen's customs of 5 percent, and the crew's one-third share. In order to meet these requirements, the value of the prizes would have to have totaled £8,824, with £882 for the lord high admiral, £441 for the queen's customs, and £2,500 for the crew.

Additionally, if the expedition produced sufficient revenues to cover the expenses of Ralegh's supply ship, it would have to have returned an additional £1,412, paying £141 to the lord high admiral, £72 to the queen's customs, and £400 to the crew. This reckoning would have left the investors an additional £800 with which to offset the cost of the supply ship. Although Ralegh is believed to have financed this vessel by himself, an accurate division of profits among Ralegh and the rest of the investors is not possible from what is presently known. They are, therefore, treated here as a group holding an undivided interest.

In the dedication of his Latin edition of Peter Martyr's *decades,* Richard Hakluyt credited Ralegh with having spent 10,000 ducats on his Virginia expeditions; this figure, converted at 6 shillings to the ducat, would represent £30,000. This sum, however, would certainly include the total investment by all parties concerned in the voyages of 1584 through 1586. If the costs of the 1584-1586 voyages are taken to amount to £20,381, it would appear that Hakluyt exaggerated the estimate of Sir Walter's investments, perhaps for the benefit of publicity.

The John White Expedition and Colony of 1587

Approximately twelve days after Sir Richard Grenville had returned from his fruitless 1586 expedition, Sir Walter Ralegh entered into an agreement with John White and the twelve men whom he had appointed assistants for the "Cittie of Ralegh in Virginea." There was scarcely sufficient time in which to formulate this new pact after Grenville's return, and, as a consequence, it is unlikely that Grenville's report had much bearing, if any, upon its terms. The charter itself no longer exists, but the document that granted a coat of arms to White, to each of his twelve assistants, and to the "Cittie of Ralegh" was issued January 7, 1587, the same date as that on which the charter was signed. It stated that Ralegh

Hath by his indenture . . . (amongste dyuers & sondry guifts, Grants & Confirmacions) nomynated elected, Chosen, Constituted made & appoynted, Iohn White of London, Gentleman, to be the chief Gouernor theare, And Roger Baylye: Ananyas

Darr: Christopher Cooper: [John Sampson: Thomas Steeuens]: William Fullwoodd, Roger Pratt, Dyonise Harvye, Iohn Nicholls, George Howe, [Iames Plat], and Symon Fardinando of London Gentleman to be Twelue Assistants, & their Successors, hath foreuer Confirmed made encorporated, & accepted one Bodye pollitique & Corporate, by the name Tytle and Aucthoritye of THE GOUERNOR AND ASSISTANTS OF THE CITTIE OF RALEGH IN VIRGINEA WITH THE/APPERTE-NANCES/. . . .

White remarked in his narrative of the 1587 expedition that Ralegh granted the colony a charter, but he gave no information as to the terms it contained. Thomas Harriot revealed in his *briefe and true report* that Ralegh had liberally granted at least 500 acres of land to each man for the adventure of his person in the enterprise. Ralegh's "liberality" possibly included financial assistance with the shipping, the cost of the stores, and other special expenses involved in developing a community, as well as the granting of bonuses to those who brought their wives and children with them. White also stated in his narrative that Ralegh personally delivered to the settlers written instructions directing them to plant the new colony on the Chesapeake Bay. Ralegh apparently retained direct control and supervision of the expedition as well as the colony and remained responsible for its conduct. Furthermore, these instructions directed White to install Manteo, after his christening, as lord of Roanoke and Dasemunkepeuc. In view of the directive that the new settlement was to be made in the Chesapeake Bay area, it is significant that Ralegh also desired to retain control over the Roanoke Island area; he may have had plans for its development in the future. By this act Ralegh assumed proprietary and feudal rights over Virginia and made Manteo his feudal subtenant. Perhaps he intended to retain a garrison there and maintain Port Ferdinando as a port of call for English ships.

From these statements by Harriot and White and the references alluded to in the document granting the coat of arms, it would appear that the colonists were to join with their financial backers and form a company that would operate under Ralegh's patents in Virginia and that both parties would share in the expenses and profits of the venture. The financial backers were to advance funds and materials, while the colonists adventured themselves and their belongings. It is presumed that both parties were to share to some degree in the financial returns derived from any minerals found or money crops raised there, which were expected to be the principal potential sources of colonial revenue.

Much less is known about the adventurers of 1587 than those of the previous colony. Grenville's interest is surmised through the remark in Pedro Diaz's deposition that Grenville, upon his return to England in 1586, had gone to London, "where he recruited people for the settlement." In a subsequent portion of the document, however, Diaz names Simon Fernandes as the "author and promoter of the venture," a surprising and not necessarily accurate statement, considering the ill will that then existed between Fernandes and Grenville.

Sir George Carey was quite probably an investor in the enterprise, not simply because of his office as vice admiral of Hampshire and governor of the Isle of Wight, from which county the expedition sailed, but also because of the 1587 privateering expedition that put to sea under Captain William Irish. Irish's ship may well have been carrying thirty-six colonists as well as their stores and provisions. Presuming such supplies were carried on board Irish's ship, the fact that the colonists of 1587 were not landed at the new settlement, as well as John White's failure to obtain additional stores in the West Indies, may help to explain the colonists' dilemma immediately after their arrival on Roanoke Island. The resulting situation prompted the settlers to seek two of their number to return to England as factors and arrange for the new supplies so urgently needed. Only White went, there being no other volunteers. White's visit to Cowes, the port adjacent to Carey's castle on the Isle of Wight, is additional circumstantial evidence of the existence of some degree of cooperation beween the settlers and Carey.

There is direct evidence, however, that William Sanderson was involved in Ralegh's financial affairs at this time, although he was undoubtedly interested in some of the prior ventures as well. On October 5, 1587, eleven days before White landed in Ireland on his return from Virginia, Ralegh and Sanderson borrowed £1,500 jointly from Thomas Smythe of London. They gave him a bond in the amount of £3,000 to cover the debt, which was cancelled by Smythe on February 4 and 5, 1591. There is no indication that the loan was repaid or for what purpose it was negotiated, although it might very well have been in connection with the Virginia enterprise. (Smythe became directly involved in the Virginia colony in 1589 under an agreement discussed later.) It is mere speculation, however, to assume that Ralegh might have been assisted by any of the 1585 adventurers in financing the 1587 agreement with White and the settlers.

The 1587 expedition was a financial disaster. Of the three vessels that put to sea, two returned, the pinnace having been left with the colonists; and of these two ships, neither captured a prize of any kind. Nor did the expedition, according to White's narrative, perform any trading or acquire in the West Indies any goods that could be sold for profit upon its return to England. The entire voyage was a drain on the resources of the investors.

The only privateering income obtained in 1587 came from the ships of Sir George Carey under Captain William Irish, which were reported to have brought to Bristol a prize worth £2,000. A customs fee of more than £230, presumably at the customary 5 percent rate, was paid on the prize and its contents. The degree of partnership or cooperation between the expeditions of Carey and Ralegh is not known; there is, therefore, no certainty that Ralegh or any other person interested in White's voyage received a share of these prize goods. But the income figure of £4,618 6s 8d is regarded as reliable, since it is derived from information taken from the records of the queen's customs.

The cost of the White expedition of 1587 can be computed on the same basis as that previously applied to the 1585 voyage. The three ships of the 1587 venture were described respectively as being 100 to 120 tons for the admiral, at least 100 tons for the flyboat, and the pinnace as being small enough to cross the bar at Port Ferdinando. The pinnaces used in the Carolina sounds in 1585 were estimated to have a capacity of from 20 to 30 tons; and, judging from Ralph Lane's caustic comments concerning the suitability of his pinnace for use in the intercoastal waters, the same type of vessel in 1587 was certainly no larger. At £4 per ton, the 1587 shipping would be valued at approximately £880 or £1,000, depending upon the size of the pinnace and taking the minimum size of the flyboat at 100 tons. Using once again the larger figure, the provisioning of these ships would double this investment, bringing the total to £2,000. At £40 per person for the outfitting of the 117 colonists who left England, the total would be increased by an additional £4,680, for a grand total of £5,680. This amount is comparable to the £9,581 figure representing the total outlay for the 1585 venture. The great difference between the costs of the two colonies arises, however, from the fact that the 1587 venture derived no revenue to offset its expense and, in addition, because the 1587 colonists appear to have shared financially in their own outfitting to some unknown degree. If such were the case, it would reduce somewhat the total investment made by Ralegh and his coadventurers.

Assuming the worst possible situation—that none of the income from Carey's ships in 1587 could be used to offset the cost of White's expedition—then the entire £5,680 cost of White's voyage must be viewed as a total loss.

The Abortive White Expedition of 1588

The 1588 expedition was also a total loss. The two pinnaces of the voyage had a total capacity of 55 tons, which, if calculated at £4 per ton, would have been worth £220. Another £220 would have to be added to cover ship stores and provisions. The fifteen colonists whom White claimed to have been carried on board would have cost an additional £600. The supplies and provisions, which were destined for the settlers, are not capable of being estimated on the basis of the information available. Discounting the quantity of these supplies, the entire expedition is likely to have cost about £1,040. The French ship that captured White's pinnace took all the provisions on board and left its crew "not at their departing any thing worth the carying away." Some of the supplies may have been salvaged from the other pinnace, which returned to England within a few weeks after the departure of White's vessel, but there is no evidence to this effect.

The "Cittie of Ralegh"

That all of these expeditions placed a strain upon Ralegh's financial resources can probably be evidenced by an agreement he made in 1589, which was entitled "An Assignment from Sir Walter Raleigh, to diuers

Gentlemen, and Merchants of London, for the inhabiting, and planting of our people in Virginia." The parties to this tripartite indenture, made on March 7, 1589, were Sir Walter Ralegh; certain merchants of London; and John White, the assistants of the "Cittie of Ralegh in Virginea," and the colonists. The merchants included, among others, William Sanderson; Walter Bayly, possibly a relative of Roger Bayly of the 1587 colony; William Gamage, possibly an ironmonger; John Gerrard, apparently the John Gerrard who composed the *Herball,* in which he acknowledged several contributions from John White; Richard Hakluyt, probably the clergyman; Thomas Hood, for whom Thomas Smythe created a mathematical lectureship in 1582; Thomas Smythe, a London merchant; and Richard Wright, haberdasher and close business associate of Thomas Smythe's son.

The roster of the assistants was changed slightly. Missing from the roster is the name of Simon Fernandes; in its place appears the name of one Humfrey Dimmocke. In return for investing in the Virginia colony "diuers & sundry sums of money, merchandises, shiping, munition, victual, and other commodities," Ralegh granted these merchants the right of free trade; the sum of £100 for their use without accountability; and immunity from all rents, subsidies, customs, taxes, duties, and the like for a period of seven years. He also assured them of his goodwill by affirming the binding nature of the contract and asserting that he would seek letters patent from the crown in order that their association might be protected by royal sanction. Ralegh meanwhile protected his own interests by reserving to himself the fifth part of any gold or silver discovered or mined in Virginia, the same amount he was legally obligated to pay to the crown.

This group of merchants, however, inherited from Ralegh liabilities rather than assets; and they do not appear to have taken any too seriously their new responsibilities toward the 1587 colony, since there is no record of their ever having dispatched an expedition in 1589 for its relief. In preparing the *Moonlight* for the 1590 expedition, Sanderson was almost certainly acting as their representative and using their contributions. Ralegh now became merely a "titular patentee," only a "nominal link" between the crown and the colonists in Virginia.

The John White Expedition of 1590

Historian David Beers Quinn is of the opinion that Ralegh was not a partner in the privateering enterprises of 1590, although he was probably interested in the expeditions of 1591, which were conducted by the same group of adventurers. The 1590 voyage consisted only of John White and up to twenty-six pieces of ordnance taken aboard one of John Watts's ships. Without knowing whether this ordnance was iron or brass cannon, it is not possible to compute its cost, even at the standard rates of about £10 per ton for iron or about £40 per ton for brass. If Sir Walter invested at all in the 1590 venture, it is most likely that he would have helped William Sanderson and his backers in financing the preparation of the *Moonlight,* although there is no documentary evidence to this effect. The *Moonlight* was an 80-ton vessel equipped with forty men and seven guns, and it would have cost perhaps £640 to put to sea. The men would normally have been paid from the profits derived from prizes taken during the voyage; however, court cases that ensued after the return of the 1590 ships to England reveal that the one great prize taken, the *Buen Jesus,* a 300- to 350-ton vice admiral of the Spanish squadron, was awarded by the High Court of Admiralty to John Watts and that it was worth £5,806 10*s* 4*d.*

Watts may have purchased whatever interest Sanderson claimed in the *Buen Jesus;* such a possibility can be surmised from the fact that the two men had at least a verbal consortship agreement and that the *Moonlight* was present and participated in the capture of the *Buen Jesus.* No other prizes are known to have been captured by Sanderson's ship. If Ralegh assisted Sanderson in financing the *Moonlight* and Watts acquired Sanderson's claim to the *Buen Jesus,* it is possible that Ralegh may have received something on his investment. Sanderson, in this case, could probably be better described as an opportunist rather than an investor in the Roanoke voyages. Therefore, the best that could be justifiably claimed on behalf of Ralegh and Sanderson is that the voyage broke even on its £640 cost. With the sale of their interest in the *Buen Jesus* to Watts, Ralegh and Sanderson would probably have avoided the customary fees.

Financial Balance Sheet, 1584-1590

Pulling together the rather general figures derived from the foregoing analysis, a balance sheet of estimated expeditures, revenues, and profits can be constructed. These figures, to be sure, have little validity other than enabling one to gain, from existing records and recorded cost figures of the period, an insight into the probable costs of sponsoring expeditions such as those known to have sailed. From the records available, it is also possible to reconstruct some general idea of the income derived from the prizes returned from these voyages.

Additionally, it is well to keep in mind that some of the ships were used in more than one voyage and that all ships' costs, calculated at the rate of £4 per ton for used shipping, had a recoverable value upon their return to England. Table 3 indicates the total estimated value of all shipping used between 1584 and 1590, and Table 4 reflects the financial balance sheet, with the recovered value of shipping added back in as a final upward adjustment of the net profits realized.

Table 3
SHIPS OF THE ROANOKE VOYAGES, 1584-1590

EXPEDITION	SHIPS	POSSIBLE IDENTIFICATION	TONNAGE	NEW VALUE (in pounds sterling)	USED VALUE (in pounds sterling)
1584 Amadas & Barlowe	bark	*Bark Ralegh*	200		800
	bark	*Dorothy*	50		200
1585 Grenville	*Tiger*		150		600
	Roebuck		140		560
	Lion		120		480
	Dorothy		40		160
	Elizabeth		40		160
	pinnace		20	125	
	pinnace		20	125	
1585 Bernard Drake	*Golden Royal*		110		440
	Job		70		280
1586 Supply Ship Greenville	ship	*Lion*	100		400
	ship	*Roebuck*	120		480
	ship	Spanish frigate prize	100		400
	ship		60		240
	ship		60		240
	ship		60		240
1587 White	*Lion*		120		480
	flyboat		100		400
	pinnace		30		120
1588 White	*Brave* (pinnace)		30		120
	Roe (pinnace)		25		100
1590 White	*Moonlight*		80		320
			1,845	250	7,220

93

Table 4
FINANCIAL BALANCE SHEET, 1584-1590
(In 1584-1590 pounds sterling)

DATE	VOYAGE	COST	TOTAL REVENUE	ADMIRALTY	QUEEN'S CUSTOMS	ONE-THIRD CREW SHARE	NET PROFIT TO OWNER/VICTUALLER
1584	Amadas & Barlowe	2,000	-0-	-0-	-0-	-0-	(2,000)
1585	Grenville/Lane	9,581	51,400	5,140	2,570	14,563	19,545
1585	Bernard Drake	3,000	20,000	2,000	1,000	5,666	8,333
1586	Ralegh supply ship	800	1,412	141	72	400	-0-
1586	Grenville	5,000	8,824	882	441	2,500	-0-
1587	White	5,680	-0-	-0-	-0-	-0-	(5,680)
1588	White (aborted)	1,040	-0-	-0-	-0-	-0-	(1,040)
1590	White/Watts	640	640	–	–	–	–
		27,741	82,276	8,163	4,083	23,129	19,158

Total recovered value of shipping costs, 1584-1590 . . . . 7,380*

Total net profits estimated, 1584-1590 26,538

---

*This sum was derived by multiplying 1,845, the total tonnage of shipping used, 1584-1590, as indicated in Table 3, by the £4-per-ton average cost of used shipping. The resulting figure could be somewhat less, however, if one or more of the ships listed in Table 3 made more than one crossing. Depreciation might also lower the value of a used ship if the vessel's condition were less than average after several voyages.

Sir Walter Ralegh's Personal Financial Involvement

Some contemporary estimates of the expenses incurred by Sir Walter Ralegh by reason of these several ventures have been made; and, although attributed to Ralegh personally, the amounts mentioned must actually represent the investments of all the Virginia adventurers. For instance, Martin Basanier estimated the cost of the 1584 and 1585 voyages to be £20,000. This figure appears to be rather high when compared to the estimated £14,581 cost for those same voyages as indicated by Table 4, especially if it is ascribed to Ralegh as his personal share. Richard Hakluyt's valuation of the cost of the voyages through February 22, 1587, was 100,000 ducats, or £30,000 at contemporary exchange rates. David Quinn suggests that this sum surely represents the outlay of funds for 1584-1586, although it undoubtedly exaggerated the actual expenditures.

It is, therefore, believed that a sum such as £30,000 represents a high but possible estimate of the total cost of the expeditions of the years 1584 to 1587 inclusive. It should also be kept in mind, however, that the documents in which these figures appear were designed as propaganda measures on behalf of Ralegh's colonizing scheme and may well have exaggerated his expenses in the different ventures.

Throughout the eighteenth, nineteenth, and twentieth centuries, numerous biographers and historians writing about Sir Walter Ralegh or the Roanoke voyages have stated that Ralegh was reputed to have expended £40,000 on these various expeditions. At his trial in 1603 Sir Walter claimed to have spent £40,000 in the service of his queen against Spain. The earliest printed reference applying this sum as an exclusive expediture of the Virginia voyages appears to be in a footnote, probably added by the unidentified editor or publisher "W.T." to a pamphlet by Sir Walter Ralegh's son, Carew Ralegh, entitled *A Brief Relation of Sir Walter Raleigh's Troubles* (1669). This footnote makes the simple assertion that "Sir Walter Raleigh discovered Virginia at his own charge, which cost him forty thousand pounds." In 1736 William Oldys first included the statement in a published biography of Ralegh, which he wrote as an introduction to a new edition of Ralegh's *Historie of the World.* And it seems to have been repeated over and over since that time. It is extremely unlikely that Carew Ralegh would have misconstrued his father's statement and placed the comment in a footnote when he was otherwise discussing his father's affairs in a very detailed manner. Furthermore, it is inconsistent with the character of the author's style. The wording of the assertion is more suggestive of an editorial insertion than of a marginal note by Ralegh's son, writing about a subject that had exerted such a profound influence on his life.

It should also be noted here that, even though it is not now possible to isolate Sir Walter Ralegh's personal investment in these ventures, there appear to have been other voyages in which he was interested that produced some handsome revenues for him. For example, he was apparently one of twelve investors in a 1592 expedition that resulted in the capture of a ship carrying bullion and goods estimated to be worth £31,150, the profits from which may have been as much as £14,952 divided among twelve persons. Therefore, whatever income was derived from this and other ventures, it is reasonably certain that Sir Walter Ralegh did not bring his personal fortunes to ruin upon the sandbars and pine forests of Elizabethan Virginia. His reverses actually began with his secret marriage to Elizabeth Throckmorton, one of Queen Elizabeth's ladies-in-waiting. This so displeased the queen when she discovered the fact in 1592 that she imprisoned Ralegh in the Tower of London. Additionally, it appears that Sir Walter was interested in other voyages in quest of the Lost Colony even as late as 1602, when one of his sea captains, Samuel Mace, was reported to be searching along the shores of Virginia.

There must also have been numerous administrative expenses of which there are no records remaining. For instance, Martin White, Ralegh's factor at Plymouth, was employed for an undetermined amount of time in preparation for the Roanoke voyages, and the salary White commanded is likewise unknown. What was the total sum of money spent by Ralegh in traveling between London and the West Country? How many pounds were spent in fees to various officials in order to obtain legal documents or to take possession of certain supplies granted by the crown? What was the cost to Ralegh of maintaining Thomas Harriot as a member of his household during the period 1584-1590? Undoubtedly, much was spent unrecorded and unremembered. Whatever Sir Walter Ralegh actually expended or profited from the Roanoke voyages, recorded or unrecorded, he appears never to have forgotten his Lost Colonists in Virginia.

1585 Pounds Sterling: A Relative View

In order to gain some perspective as to the contemporary value of the total expenditures of £27,741 for the 1584-1590 voyages, or of the net profit of £26,538 apparently gained from them (see Table 4, p. 94), it is somewhat instructive to compare these sums with the annual income of an average citizen of that period. For example, the average annual wage of a carpenter in 1585 was about £15. This means that Sir Walter Ralegh and his associates expended during a seven-year period about 264.2 times the wages a carpenter might have earned during the same time. Likewise, it would mean that they netted a profit of about 252.7 times the expected earnings of a carpenter. The annual income of an average family in 1585 was about £16; this figure would, of course, yield a very similar ratio.

During the seven years, Ralegh and his associates appear to have averaged a 95.7 percent return on their investment, all of it derived from revenues accrued during one year, 1585. The remaining six years were a total loss or at best netted a very small amount through the recovery of ship costs from the returning vessels. Such risky schemes might not please modern-day investors, who routinely rely upon federal insurance guarantees of their personal savings accounts. Compared to the present-day investor, Ralegh and his associates operated in virtually a total-risk environment. Their chances of immediate return were predicated upon finding in Virginia local exportable wealth, which they first had to discover; upon developing money crops that could provide the basis for a profitable trade, a long-term investment proposition at best; or upon confiscating Spanish bullion and cargo on the high seas, which, even with royal sanction, was a very risky business. One had not only to find a ship bearing a rich cargo but also to approach it under circumstances that would provide a good chance of success. This did not always happen, as evidenced, for instance, by the 1588 voyages.

Therefore, the fickle fortunes of fate, which granted a great prize or two in one year and nothing but disappointments in another, obviously cooled the ardor of many of Ralegh's associates who invested in the colonial enterprise. The London merchants, who were given a partnership role in the venture in 1589, evidently did not think there was sufficient promise of a desirable return on their investment to remain involved and support the effort. This is not to say that they did not invest in privateering ventures, for they did. And great was their profit. It is perhaps reasonable to assume, however, that the London merchants did not share Ralegh's commitment to the establishment of a British empire, a motivation that guided his thoughts and aspirations. Consequently, they probably saw little compelling reason to share their profits from successful privateering voyages with colonizing expeditions, which seemed only to absorb funds and gave little indication of any realistic return in the short term. Perhaps the idea of colonization was still too new in the English experience to be acceptable to those who could afford the investment.

In 1590, however, it was only seventeen years until the Jamestown colony was planted on the shores of the James River in present-day Virginia, not far away from the place where the Lost Colony of 1587 was supposed to have been established.

IX. Conclusion

The predominant force behind the Roanoke voyages of 1584-1590 was Sir Walter Ralegh, who was motivated by his vision of an overseas empire capable of generating enormous material wealth and international political power for England, surpassing even that of Spain. Not all Englishmen, however, shared with Ralegh his confidence in this eventual reality. When Sir Walter's limited funds forced him to seek the financial assistance essential for implementing his plans, few men of means were willing to cooperate with him. This reluctance was undoubtedly attributable to the long-term nature of the investment required in establishing a colony and the sizable reserves necessary to send annual supply expeditions until the colony could achieve economic stability. The only sources of immediate returns anticipated from such investments were from any rich minerals that might be discovered in the colony or from prize goods and bullion taken through privateering, which was actually a legitimate although undeclared form of warfare on the high seas.

In this painting by Darrell McClure the Indians witness a pivotal moment in history as they watch the arrival of the English in their large wooden ships gliding silently before the wind.

Privateering was intended to serve as a motivating factor for attracting investors in colonial enterprises; however, this same motivation often militated against Ralegh's ultimate goal of establishing a permanent colony in the New World. The prevailing concern for the capture of Spanish treasure was the cause for violating Ralegh's instructions that the 1587 colony be established on the shores of Chesapeake Bay. It was likewise responsible for the failure of the 1588 and 1590 expeditions insofar as they were engaged in the supply and relief of that unfortunate group of settlers. The desire for gold also seemed to preoccupy the minds and energies of Ralph Lane's men in the 1585 colony. With the example of Central American wealth paraded across the oceans every year to fill the coffers of the Spanish crown, it is difficult to blame them.

An effort has been made in the foregoing chapters to describe the means by which Ralegh procured the supplies and equipment necessary to establish his Roanoke colonies; the lofty caliber of the men with whom he surrounded himself as well as the generally superior qualities of those persons whom he chose to participate as colonists or members of expeditions; and Sir Walter's personal friendship with Queen Elizabeth I, from whom was derived the fortune that enabled him to launch such ambitious colonizing schemes.

A suggestion has been presented that from the combined voyages made between 1584 and 1590, a profit of a substantial nature was most certainly realized by the collective group of adventurers who invested in the expeditions, although the personal balance sheet of any one of these men, Sir Walter Ralegh included, has not been discernible from the small number of existing records. The records that do exist are tantalizing enough with their innuendos and implications. As newly discovered document collections or newly released collections of private papers are made available and studied for the first time, new evidence is continuously being revealed. Imperfect impressions are consistently being revised to new levels of understanding.

That Ralegh was pursuing a dream is not to be denied; but it was a dream with a highly practical, long-range objective, an objective he appears always to have kept firmly in mind. Through the preparations he undertook for the Virginia voyages, he proved himself in the long run to be not only a statesman of vision but also a politician with a keen eye for personal profit and an alert mind for turning adverse situations to his own advantage.

But the dividing line between a man of vision and a visionary is one of very fine distinction. For Ralegh also revealed himself in the short term to be something of a visionary, dreaming dreams greater than the more limited and mundane objectives of his associates permitted them to comprehend. He was, perhaps, too engrossed in an idea and the impact it could have upon his world to plan in realistic fashion an adequate economic environment in which the idea could thrive and endure. Perhaps he misunderstood the real motives of his fellow investors. Perhaps he relied too extensively upon political influences and alliances, which have a peculiar habit of fading into the shadows of passing years.

If Ralegh's associates participated in his expeditions in anticipation of sharing in those riches they hoped would be discovered in Virginia or captured upon the high seas, it is no wonder that their ardor cooled. Only the expeditions of 1585 showed any profit, and what a profit that was! After the losses sustained by the voyages of 1586-1590, however, only Ralegh and his kindred spirit, Richard Hakluyt, the cleric, remained steadfast, continuing to dream of the glories of an English empire overseas and the wealth and power it would one day bring home to England.

One thing has remained constant, however: there does not appear to be any diminishing interest over the ensuing centuries in any phase of Ralegh's varied activities, especially those concerning Roanoke Island, as evidenced by the large number of volumes that have been written on the subject. Sir Walter Ralegh and his dream of an "Inglishe nation" still hold a commanding position on center stage as Americans chart a course into their own future while keeping a weather eye from whence they came.

APPENDIX A
GENEALOGICAL REFERENCE CHART

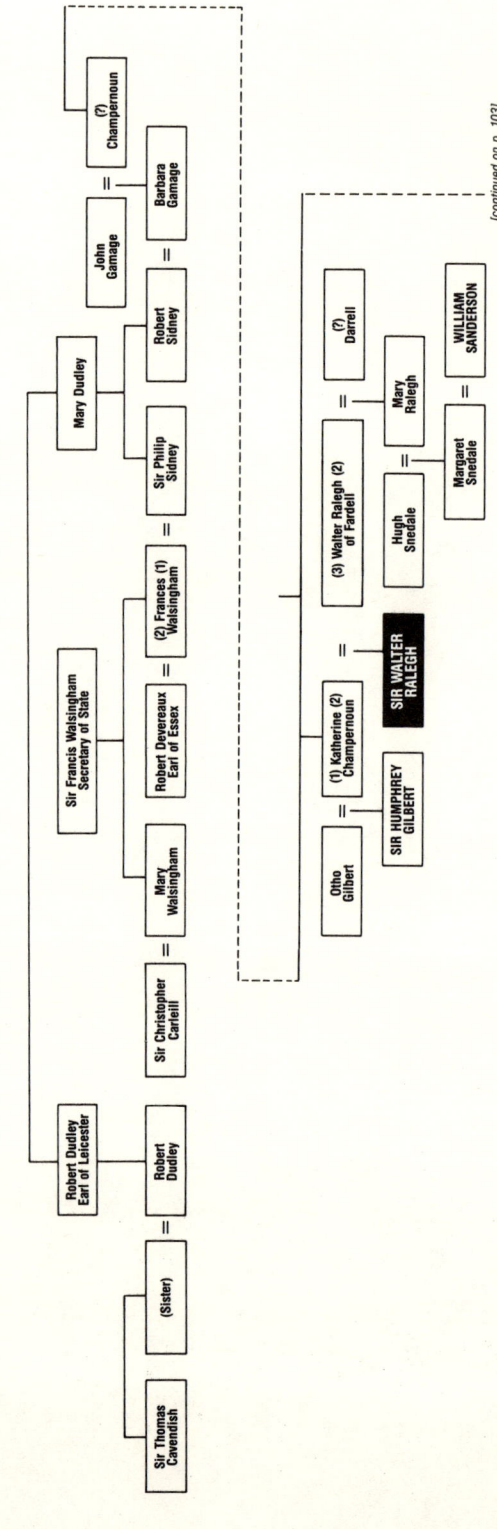

[continued on p. 103]

102

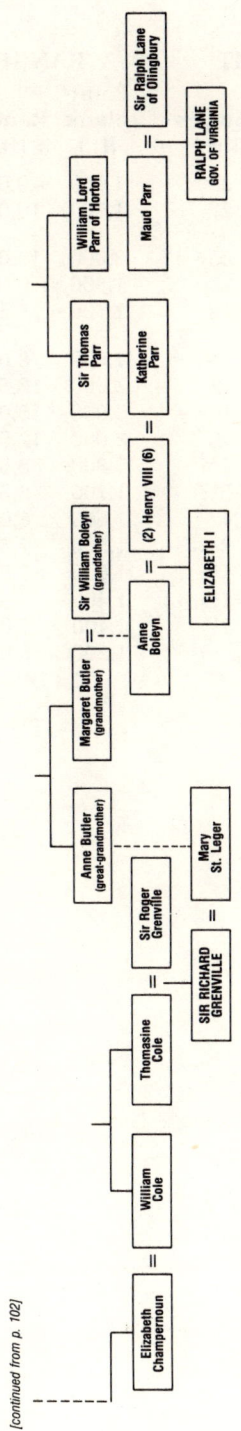

This simplified genealogical chart illustrates how Sir Walter Ralegh was aligned either by blood or marriage with many of the prominent and influential families of Elizabethan times.

Perhaps the key person in this family maze was Ralegh's mother, Katherine Champernoun. By a previous marriage, she had provided her son a connection with the well-known Gilberts, Sir Humphrey Gilbert being the original holder of the queen's patents to colonize the New World—patents that Ralegh was later granted. It was through a previous marriage of Sir Walter Ralegh's father that the connection was made with William Sanderson, who assisted Sir Walter with some of the financing of the Roanoke voyages.

Katherine Champernoun, herself descended from an illustrious family, had two sisters who made other connections possible for Sir Walter Ralegh. One sister had a daughter, Barbara Gamage, whose marriage to Robert Sidney was apparently arranged by Sir Walter. This brought into the family fold such powerful public personalities as Sir Francis Walsingham, the secretary of state; Sir Christopher Carleill, a contender with Ralegh to inherit Sir Humphrey Gilbert's patents to colonize the New World; Robert Deveraux, earl of Essex, and Robert Dudley, earl of Leicester, both court favorites of the queen; and Thomas Cavendish, both a contributor to and a member of the 1585 expedition. Elizabeth Champernoun, another sister of Katherine, provided an equally remarkable connection through her marriage to the uncle of Sir Richard Grenville, general of the 1585 expedition. Through Sir Richard's wife can be traced an interesting connection to Queen Elizabeth herself, although it was much too remote to be exploited for royal favors. Elizabeth's connection to Ralph Lane was acknowledged, however, since she referred to him as her kinsman.

103

APPENDIX B
STANDARD GUNS OF THE ELIZABETHAN ERA

NAME	BORE		WEIGHT		RANGE	
		Weapon	Shot	Powder	Point-blank	Random
	(Inches)	(lbs.)	(lbs.)	(lbs.)	(ft.)	(ft.)
Cannon Royal	8½	8,000	66	30	1,600	9,650
Cannon	8	6,000	60	27	1,700	10,000
Cannon Serpentine	7½	5,500	53½	25	2,000	10,000
Bastard Cannon	7	4,500	41	20	1,800	9,000
Demi Cannon	6¾	4,000	30½	18	1,700	8,500
Perier Cannon (Stone Cannon)	6	3,000	24½	14	1,600	8,000
Culverin	5½	4,500	17½	12	2,000	12,500
Basilisk	5	4,000	15½	10	2,000	15,000
Demi Culverin	4½	3,400	9½	8	2,000	12,500
Bastard Culverin	4	3,000	7	5¾	1,800	8,500
Saker	3½	1,400	5½	5½	1,700	8,500
Minion	3¼	1,000	4	4	1,600	8,000
Falcon	2½	600	2¼	2¼	1,500	7,500
Falconet	2	500	1½	1½	1,500	7,500
Fowler	1¾	450	1	1½	1,400	—
Serpentine	1½	400	¾	1½	1,400	7,000
Robinet	1	300	½	⅓	1,200	5,000

APPENDIX C
GLOSSARY OF TERMS PERTAINING TO
SHIPS AND WEAPONRY

The following definitions apply to various terms used in the text.

BARK. Originally a term used to describe any small sailing ship of any type of rigging. By the sixteenth century it was usually a three-masted ship with foremasts and mainmasts square-rigged and the mizzenmast lateen-rigged with fore-and-aft mounting.

BILL. A long-shafted hook and blade combination, sometimes called a bill hook

CALIVER. An early handgun

CARRACK. A large trading vessel of northern and southern Europe used between the fourteenth and seventeenth centuries. It was the forerunner of the three-masted ship, which, itself, was the major influence in naval architecture until the advent of steam power in the nineteenth century. Carracks were the first vessels to carry guns. In northern Europe they were square-rigged, and in the Mediterranean area they were lateen-rigged. They were eventually constructed as large as 1,200 tons.

CORSELET. Armor covering the front and back of the upper part of the body

FLYBOAT. A flat-bottomed Dutch coastal vessel with a high and ornately decorated stern. It had one or two masts and was square-rigged with a spritsail.

GALLEASS. This ship design was a hybrid between a galley and a galleon. It was as much as 150 feet in length, with a 25-foot beam and two or three masts. It was fitted with one bank of oars and lateen sails. Mostly used to haul freight, it was introduced as a style of warship but was short lived as a nautical design. It had nearly disappeared by 1600.

HALBERD. A pike and battle-ax combination mounted on a shaft, usually about 6 feet long

HARQUEBUS. An early version of a musket. It was propped on a support staff while fired from the shoulder.

LIGHT HORSEMAN. A long, light wherry capable of being carried in sections aboard a larger ship

LIGHTER. A barge without its own means of propulsion, usually towed by another vessel and used to carry freight between ship and shore

MORION. A helmet without a visor but with a curved brim coming to an upturned point in the front and rear

PARTISAN. A broad-bladed pike or modified halberd

PIKE. A metal spearhead on a wooden shaft

PINNACE. Normally a two-masted square-rigged ship of about 20 tons. It was often used as an "advice boat," carrying messages between ships. It varied in size, some being small enough to be towed behind larger ships as boats and others being large enough to be assigned permanent crews of their own.

SAILS: *Lateen.* A four-sided sail hung fore and aft on the mast with a lug or gaff (short stay) angled upward from the top and a horizontal foot or bottom stay

Square. A four-sided sail hung from a yard set square, or at right angles, with the mast. Most English ships of the sixteenth century were square-riggers.

Sprit. A small square sail set on square riggers held in place by a sprit, a spar that ran fore and aft from the base of the mast diagonally across to the upper corner of the sail opposite

SHALLOP. A small, fast vessel of about 25 tons, often used as a tender for larger warships. Shallops usually had only one mast, which was lug-rigged. Sometimes they were small enough to be carried aboard larger ships. They were replaced by the longboat in the seventeenth century. Shallop was also a term used to describe a boat built on some foreign shore from timbers of a shipwreck in an attempt by a crew to return home. Such a vessel was usually undecked.

TILTBOAT. This term was often used to describe a boat with an awning mounted on it to protect passengers from the bright sun or other elements of the weather. It was commonly used as a ferryboat for passengers on the Thames River between London and other nearby places. The term could also refer to a wherry with an awning mounted on it.

WHERRY. An oared boat used for carrying passengers. It was perhaps 14 feet long, with a rudder and at least one rower. A double-oared wherry would be expected to have four oars. It was often thought of as a gentleman's boat and was particularly associated with the Thames River.

Bibliographic References for Additional Reading

Adams, Randolph G. "An Effort to Identify John White." *American Historical Review,* XII (October, 1935), 87-91.

Andrews, Kenneth R. *Elizabethan Privateering, 1585-1603.* Cambridge, England: Cambridge University Press, 1964.

Andrews, Kenneth R., ed. *English Privateering Voyages, 1588-1603.* Cambridge, England: Hakluyt Society, 1959.

Cumming, William. "The Identity of John White Governor of Roanoke and John White the Artist." *North Carolina Historical Review,* XV (July, 1938), 197-203.

Cumming, William P., R. A. Skelton, and David Beers Quinn. *The Discovery of North America.* New York: American Heritage Press, 1972.

Detweiler, Robert. "Was Richard Hakluyt a Negative Influence in the Colonization of Virginia?" *North Carolina Historical Review,* XLVIII (October, 1971), 356-369.

Edwards, Edward. *The Life of Sir Walter Ralegh.* N.p.: Macmillan Company, 2 volumes, 1868.

Glasgow, Thomas M., Jr. "HMS *Tiger.*" *North Carolina Historical Review,* XLIII (April, 1966), 115-121.

Greenblatt, Stephen Jay. *Sir Walter Ralegh, the Renaissance Man and His Roles.* New Haven: Yale University Press, 1973.

Hariot, Thomas. *A Briefe and True Report of the New Found Land of Virginia.* New York: Dover Publications, 1972. (A reprint of the English edition of Theodor de Bry's *America,* Part I [Frankfurt-am-Main, 1590]).

Harrington, Jean Carl. "The Manufacture and Use of Bricks at the Raleigh Settlement on Roanoke Island." *North Carolina Historical Review,* XLIV (January, 1967), 1-17.

_____ . *Search for the Cittie of Raleigh.* Washington, D.C.: National Park Service, 1962.

Lacey, Robert. *Sir Walter Ralegh.* New York: Atheneum, 1974.

Lorant, Stefan. *The New World.* New York: Duell, Sloan and Pearce, 1946.

Morison, Samuel Eliot. *The European Discovery of America: The Northern Voyages.* New York: Oxford University Press, 1971.

Parks, George Bruner. *Richard Hakluyt and the English Voyages.* New York: American Geographical Society, 1928.

Powell, William S. "Roanoke Colonists and Explorers: An Attempt at Identification." *North Carolina Historical Review,* XXXIV (April, 1957), 202-226.

Quinn, David Beers. *England and the Discovery of America, 1481-1620.* New York: Alfred A. Knopf, 1974.

_____ . *Raleigh and the British Empire.* New York: Collier Books, revised edition, 1962.

Quinn, David Beers, ed. *The Roanoke Voyages, 1584-1590.* Cambridge, England: Cambridge University Press, 2 volumes, 1955.

Quinn, David Beers, and Alison M. Quinn. *The First Colonists.* Raleigh: Division of Archives and History, North Carolina Department of Cultural Resources, 1982.

Quinn, David B., Alison M. Quinn, and Susan Sutton, eds. *New American World: A Documentary History of North America to 1612.* New York: Arno Press and Hector Bye, 5 volumes, 1979. (Volume III of this work contains many of the Roanoke documents as well as several additions that have appeared since *The Roanoke Voyages* was published.)

Rowse, A. L. *The Elizabethans and America.* New York: Harper Brothers, 1959.

_____ . *The Expansion of Elizabethan England.* New York: St. Martin's Press, 1955.

_____ . *Sir Richard Grenville of the Revenge.* Boston: Houghton, Mifflin Co., 1937.

Rukeyser, Muriel. *The Traces of Thomas Hariot.* New York: Random House, 1971.

Sams, Conway Whittle. *The Conquest of Virginia: The First Attempt.* Norfolk, Virginia: Keyser-Doherty Printing Corporation, 1924.

Shirley, John W., ed. *Thomas Harriot: Renaissance Scientist.* Oxford, England: Clarendon Press, 1974.

Smith, Lacey Baldwin. *The Horizon Book of the Elizabethan World.* New York: American Heritage Publishing Co., 1967.

Winton, John. *Sir Walter Ralegh.* New York: Coward McCann and Geohegan, 1975.

Wright, Irene A., ed. *Further English Voyages to Spanish America, 1583-1594.* London: Hakluyt Society, 1951.